Truth and Beauty

Aesthetics and Motivations in Science

Truth and Beauty

Aesthetics and Motivations in Science

S. Chandrasekhar

The University of Chicago Press

CHICAGO AND LONDON

S. CHANDRASEKHAR is the Morton D. Hull Distinguished Service Professor
Emeritus in the Department of Astronomy and Astrophysics, the Department of Physics, and the Enrico Fermi Institute at the University of Chicago. He has received many awards in his career, including the Nobel Prize
for physics, the National Medal of Science (U.S.), and the Copley Medal of
the Royal Society (London). He is the author of *An Introduction to the Study of
Stellar Structure, Principles of Stellar Dynamics, Radiative Transfer, Hydrodynamic
and Hydromagnetic Stability, Ellipsoidal Figures of Equilibrium, The Mathematical
Theory of Black Holes, Eddington: The Most Distinguished Astrophysicist of His
Time,* and *Plasma Physics.*

The University of Chicago Press, Chicago 60637
The University of Chicago Press, Ltd., London

LIBRARY OF CONGRESS CATALOGING IN PUBLICATION DATA

Chandrasekhar, S. (Subrahmanyan), 1910–
  Truth and beauty.

  1. Science—Aesthetics. 2. Physics—Philosophy.
3. Motivation (Psychology) 4. Milne, Edward Arthur,
1896–1950. 5. Eddington, Arthur Stanley, Sir,
1882–1944. 6. Schwarzschild, K. (Karl), 1873–1916,
I. Title
Q175.C453 1987   530'.01   87-13792
ISBN 0-226-10086-3

Contents

Preface

The seven lectures collected in this volume present my general thoughts pertaining to the motivations in the pursuit of science and to the patterns of scientific creativity. While the first of these lectures was given forty years ago (under a special circumstance I shall presently describe), the remaining six were given in the decade following 1975. As such, they may illustrate the changing (maturing?) attitudes of one scientist.

All of the lectures were prepared with care and attention to details and phrasing. They were, in fact, read on the occasions; the printed lectures are the unaltered original texts (apart from the elimination of some "preliminary" material).

I

The lectures fall in, roughly, two categories. The first four deal primarily with questions of aesthetics and motivations. The remaining three lectures, bearing the names of Milne, Eddington, and Schwarzschild, while in part biographical, do address themselves, albeit indirectly, to the same general questions; and especially the Karl Schwarzschild lecture, in which the larger part is addressed to the aesthetic base of the general theory of relativity and continues the arguments of the earlier lecture on "Beauty and the Quest for Beauty in Science."

II

The span of thirty years that separates my lecture on "The Scientist" given in 1946 and the second Nora and Edward Ryerson Lecture on "Shakespeare, Newton, and Beethoven, or Patterns of Creativity" given in 1975, is, as I have stated, the result of a special circumstance. Scientists, as a rule, do not regard motivations in the pursuit of science or the aesthetic base for such pursuits as subjects worthy of serious discussion; and they tend to look askance at those who do. I probably shared these common views in 1945. But a letter from Robert Maynard Hutchins (then the Chancellor of the University of Chicago) inviting me to give the lecture on "The Scientist" in a series he was organizing explained:

> The purpose of the lecture series is to stimulate the student's critical abilities in order to enable him to appreciate the excellence of a work, and to induce him to an attempt to produce good things himself, [with the hope] that each of the lecturers will speak from his own experience on the work of his art or profession, and that he will demonstrate its value by elucidating its nature, formulating its purpose, and explaining its techniques.

I was, in the first instance, reluctant to accept the invitation: I had not given any serious thought to such matters. Besides, I was intimidated by the list of the other lecturers (including Frank Lloyd Wright, Arnold Schoenberg, Marc Chagall, and John von Neumann, among others) whom Hutchins had also invited. (Indeed, who would not be intimidated by such a list?) But I was too young to withstand the authority of the Chancellor of the University! And I was compelled to think on matters that were not natural for me at that time.

Rereading that lecture of forty years ago, I find much that I would not say or would say differently from my present vantage. But I have included it in the present collection (perhaps, against better judgment) since reading it in juxtaposition with the lecture on "The Pursuit of Science: Its Motivations," given in 1985, may illustrate how the attitudes of a scientist can alter over the years.

III

Chronologically, the lecture I gave after "The Scientist" was the Ryerson Lecture of 1975. A forced convalescence of some six months, in the preceding year, gave me the unique opportunity to think, undistractedly, on matters and issues that I had never seriously thought of before. Those six months of study and thought provided me the base not only for the lecture that I was to give, but also for my continuing interest in the role of aesthetic sensibility in the cultivation of science. In some respects, my increasing involvement in certain mathematical aspects of the general theory of relativity has strengthened the same interests. (I may add, parenthetically, that in some strange way, any new fact or insight that I may have found has not seemed to me as a "discovery" of mine, but rather as something that had always been there and that I had chanced to pick up.)

IV

There is a pair of intertwining threads that runs through all of the lectures given since 1975: the same illustrative "stories," in different shades of context, find their places in several of them. One of the running threads is related to the quest for beauty in science, and the other, to the question explicitly asked in my Ryerson Lecture concerning the origin of the different patterns of creativity in the arts and in the sciences. That there *is* a difference in the two patterns is brought out most clearly in the contrasting premises that commonly underlie the discussions pertaining to the works of an artist and the works of a scientist. In assessing an artist, one often distinguishes an early, a middle, and a late period; and the distinction is generally one of growing maturity and depth. But this is not the way a scientist is assessed: he (or she) is assessed by the significance of one or more of the discoveries that he (or she) may have made in the realm of ideas or in the realm of facts. And, it is often the case that the most "important" discovery of a scientist is his first. In contrast, the deepest creation of an artist is equally often his last. I continue to be puzzled by this dichotomy.

There is one aspect of this dichotomy that has recently occurred to me and to which I may briefly allude: it is the apparently differing goals of the scientists of the sixteenth and the seventeenth centuries and of the scientists of the present. Consider the supreme example of Newton. He discovered his laws of gravitation (and much else) while sojourning in Woolsthrope during the great plague. When some twenty years later, he undertook to write out afresh, for the benefit of Halley, his derivation of Kepler's first law, he did not stop with his derivation. He was not satisfied either with his lectures *De Motu Corporum in gyrum* that he gave subsequently. He had to write the entire *Principia*: and he wrote it with a speed and a coherence unparalleled in the intellectual history of man. A revealing aspect of this effort, from our present vantage point, is that Newton was not content with a bald enunciation of his discoveries: he seems to have been concerned, far more, in placing his discoveries in the context of the entire domain of science that he was able to construct and perceive as a whole. Newton's attitude in this respect was not exceptional for his times. Kepler could have been content with giving a simple account of his laws of planetary motion. He chose, instead, to write *Astronomia Nova*. Galileo could have stopped with the announcements of his great discoveries; but he, apparently, felt compelled to write his *Dialogues Concerning the Two New Sciences*. And the tradition of Kepler, Galileo, and Newton was passed on to Laplace and Lagrange.

It is of course idle for any normal person to wish to emulate, in scale or in magnitude, the examples of Newton, Kepler, and Galileo. But the examples do suggest that the goals of science, as *they* sought in their enlarged visions, might have retained currency with more modest but similar goals. But the goals changed; the emphasis became increasingly in identifying discoveries that change the directions of science. Perhaps the change was inevitable. The discoveries associated with the names of Volta, Ampère, Oersted, and Faraday, by their very nature, had to precede the synthesis by Maxwell; and they required different types of efforts. In any event, the tendency to focus on "discoveries" has continued; and it has been enhanced and emphasized by an outlook that perceives in discoveries the principal ingredients of scientific accomplishment. The value of synthesizing one's vision, even if of a limited range, in one simple mosaic has faded. We do not, for example, ask whether Einstein, twenty years after the discovery of *his* laws of gravitation, might have wished (or, felt able) to write an account of the general theory of relativity in the manner of the *Principia*.

May it not be, that had the goals of science, as sought by the great scientists of the sixteenth and the seventeenth centuries, retained their currency, the present dichotomy in the patterns of creativity of the artist and the scientist might not have arisen?

It remains to add that while preparing the lectures collected in this volume (as well as others) I have discussed in depth with my wife, Lalitha, the various issues that arise. Her critical understanding and parallel insights have contributed greatly to the final versions. I am also indebted to her for her constant encouragement and advice.

S. Chandrasekhar

8 December 1986

1

The Scientist

I must confess at the outset to a feeling of apprehension at being included in this series on "Works of the Mind," as I am deeply aware of my shortcomings to speak either with assurance or with authority on a subject as wide and comprehensive in its scope as a discussion of the creative works of the scientist must be. But while I have these misgivings about the appropriateness of my representing the scientist in this series, I have no such misgivings in the choice of astronomy and astrophysics to represent the exact sciences. For astronomy among the exact sciences is the most comprehensive of all, and perfection in its practice requires scholarship in all its many phases. In another respect also, astronomy holds a unique position among the sciences,

as it is the only branch of the ancient sciences which has come to us intact after the collapse of the Roman Empire. Of course, the level of astronomical studies dropped within the boundaries of the remnants of the Roman Empire, but the traditions of astronomical theory and practice were never lost. On the contrary, the clumsy methods of Greek trigonometry were improved by Hindu and Arabic astronomers, and new observations were constantly compared with those of Ptolemy and so on. This must be paralleled with the total loss of understanding of the higher branches of Greek mathematics before one realizes that astronomy is the most direct link connecting the modern sciences with the ancient. Indeed, the works of Copernicus, Tycho Brahe, and Kepler can be understood only by constant reference to the ancient methods

This lecture was given on 26 March 1946 as a part of The Works of the Mind lecture series sponsored by the University of Chicago. It was published in *The Works of the Mind*, ed. Robert B. Heywood (Chicago: University of Chicago Press, 1947).

and concepts, while the Greek theory of irrational magnitudes and the Archimedes method of integration were understood only after being independently discovered by the moderns. (O. Neugebauer)

The sponsors of this series have indicated that each contributor will demonstrate the value of his art or profession by elucidating its nature, formulating its purpose, and explaining its techniques. But before I discuss these questions, I want to draw your attention to one broad division of the physical sciences which has to be kept in mind: the division into a *basic* science and a *derived* science. You will notice that my distinction is not between a "pure science" and an "applied science." I shall not be concerned with the latter, as I do not believe that the true values of science are to be found in the conscious calculated pursuit of the applications of science. I shall, therefore, be concerned only with what is generally called "pure science"; it is the division of this into a basic science and a derived science that I wish to draw your attention. While an exact or a sharp division between the two domains cannot be made or maintained, that it exists all the same will become apparent from the examples I shall presently give. But, broadly speaking, we may say that basic science seeks to analyze the ultimate constitution of matter and the basic concepts of space and time. Derived science, on the other hand, is concerned with the rational ordering of the multifarious aspects of natural phenomena in terms of the basic concepts. Stated in this manner, it is evident, first, that the division is dependent on the state of science at a particular time and, second, that there may be, and indeed are, different levels in which natural phenomena can be analyzed. For example, there is the domain of the Newtonian laws in which an enormous range and variety of phenomena find their direct and natural explanation. And then there is the domain of the quantum theory in which other types of problems receive their solution. When there are such different levels of analysis, there exist criteria which will enable us to decide when one set of laws is appropriate and the other set inappropriate or clumsy, as the case may be.

But to return to the division itself, I do not believe that there exists a better example of a basic discovery than Rutherford's discovery of the large angle scattering of α-particles. The experiment he performed was quite simple. Using a source of high-energy α-particles emitted by a radioactive substance, Rutherford allowed them to fall on a thin foil and found that sometimes the α-particles were actually scattered backward—rarely but certainly. Recalling this later in his life (1936), Rutherford said: "This was quite the most incredible event that has ever happened to me in my life." He has described his immediate reactions in the following words: "It was almost as incredible as if you fired a 15-inch shell at a tissue paper and it bounced back and hit you." He further records:

> On consideration I soon realized that this scattering backwards must be the result of a single collision, and when I made calculations I saw that it was impossible to get anything of that order of magnitude unless you took a system in which the greater part of the mass of the atom was concentrated in a minute nucleus. It was then that I had the idea of an atom with a minute massive center carrying a charge. I worked out mathematically what laws scattering should obey, and I found that the number of particles scattered through a given angle should be proportional to the thickness of the foil, the square of the nuclear charge, and inversely proportional to the fourth power of the velocity. These deductions were later verified by Geiger and Marsden in a series of beautiful experiments.

And so it was that the nuclear model of the atom, which is at the basis of all science, was born. A single observation and its correct interpretation led to a revolution in scientific thought unparalleled in the annals of science.

I would suppose that the discovery of the neutron by Chadwick is in the same category, as it is now believed that these together with protons are the basic constituents of all nuclei. But you should not suppose from these two examples that all basic scientific facts are necessarily to be gathered only in the field of atomic physics. Indeed, the first example of a law which may be called "basic" is astronomical in origin. I refer to the discovery by Kepler of the laws of planetary motion after long and patient analysis of the extensive observations of Tycho Brahe. These laws of Kepler led Newton to his celebrated laws of gravitation, which occupied the central scientific arena for over two hundred years. I shall return to this matter presently in a somewhat different context, but the example suffices to indicate that only in the gravitational domain can astronomy lead directly to results of a basic character. A further illustration of this is the fact that the minute departures exhibited by the motion of the planet Mercury from the predictions based on Newtonian laws indicated and later confirmed the far-reaching changes in our concept of space and time implied by the general theory of relativity. In the same way, it is not impossible that the discovery by Hubble of the recession of extragalactic nebulae with velocities proportional to their distances may lead to further modifications in our basic concepts.

The examples which I have just given might suggest that the true values of science are to be found in those pursuits which lead directly to advances which I have termed "basic." Indeed, there are many physicists who seriously take this view. For example, a very distinguished physicist, apparently feeling sorry for my preoccupation with things astronomical and with an intent to cheering me, said that I should really have been a physicist. To my mind this attitude represents a misunderstanding of the real values of science. And the history of science contradicts it. From the time of Newton to the beginning of this century, the whole science of dynamics and its derivative celestial mechanics have consisted entirely in amplification, in elaboration, and in working out the consequences of the laws of Newton. Halley, Laplace, Lagrange, Hamilton, Jacobi, Poincaré—all of them were content to spend a large part of their scientific efforts in doing exactly this, that is, in the furtherance of a derived science. A derision of the derived aspects of science, implying as it would a denial of the values which these men have so earnestly sought, is to my mind sufficiently absurd to merit further consideration. Indeed, it must be apparent to an impartial observer that there is a complementary relationship between the basic and the derived aspects of science. The basic concepts gain their validity in proportion to the extent of the domain of natural phenomena which can be analyzed in terms of them. And, in limiting the domain of validity of these concepts, we recognize the operation of other laws more general than those we have operated with. Looked at in this way, science is a perpetual becoming, and it is in sharing its progress in common effort that the values of science are achieved. With these remarks, I think that I may state in a more formal manner what I regard as the true values of science which a scientist in the practice of his profession seeks to attain.

Scientific values consist in the continual and increasing recognition of the uniformity of nature. In practice this only means that the values are attained in a larger or smaller measure in extending, or equivalently limiting, the domain of applicability of our concepts relating to matter, space, and time. In other words, a scientist seeks continually to extend the domain of validity of certain basic concepts. In so doing, he attempts to discover the limitations, if any, of these same concepts, and in this way he tries to formulate concepts of wider scope and generality. These values which are the quest of a scientist take in practice one of three distinct forms which I shall discuss under the headings: "Universality of the Basic Laws," "Predictions Based on the Basic Laws," and "Identifications Resulting from the Basic Laws."

Let me illustrate each of these by some examples.

In some ways the universality of the laws of nature is best illustrated by showing how this was achieved with regard to the law of gravitation.

It is found that, all over the earth, objects are attracted toward the center of the earth. How far does this tendency go? Can it reach as far as the moon? These were the questions which Newton asked himself and answered. Galileo had already shown that uniform motion is as natural as rest and that deviation from such motion must imply a force. If, then, the moon were relieved of all forces, it would leave its orbit and go off along the instantaneous tangent to the orbit. Consequently, if the motion of the moon is due to the attraction of the earth, then what the attraction really does is to draw the moon out of the tangent into the orbit. As the period and the distances of the moon are known, it is easy to compute how much the moon falls away from the tangent in one second. Comparing this with the speed of falling bodies on the earth, Newton found the ratio of the two speeds to be about as 1 to 3600. As the moon is sixty times as far from the center of the earth as we are, this implies a force that decreases with the square of the distance.

The next question Newton asked himself was how universal this property is. In particular, does a similar force reside in the sun, keeping the planets in their orbits as the earth does the moon? The answer is to be found in Kepler's laws. Newton showed that Kepler's second law—that planets describe equal areas in equal times—implies a *central force*, that is, a force directed toward the sun; that the first law—that the planetary orbits are ellipses with the sun at one focus—is a consequence of the inverse square law of attraction; and, finally, if the same law holds from planet to planet, then the periods and distances should be related as in Kepler's third law. It was in this manner that Newton was able to announce his law of gravitation that every particle in the universe attracts every other particle with a force that varies inversely as the square of their distance apart and directly as the masses of the two particles. You will notice the use of the word "universe" in this formulation and the clear indication that its importance arises from its universality.

One further related observation. In 1803 William Herschel was able to announce from his study of close pairs of stars that in some instances the pairs represented real physical binaries, revolving in orbits about each other. Herschel was further able to show that the apparent orbits were ellipses and that Kepler's law of areas was also valid. In other words, this observation extended the validity of the laws of gravitation from the solar system to the distant stars. It is difficult for us to imagine how tremendous the impression was which this discovery of Herschel made on his contemporaries.

A good deal of the progress of astronomy since Newton's laws were announced had been concerned with their application to the motions in the solar system. Newton himself pointed out many of their chief consequences. To mention only two of these, he found the correct explanation for the phenomenon of ocean tides, and also for the precession of the equinoxes, a phenomenon which had been discovered twenty centuries earlier by Hipparchus.

The application of Newton's laws throughout the solar system is a task of incredible difficulty and one that has taxed the powers of such giants as Lagrange, Laplace, Euler, Adams, Delaunay, Hill, Newcomb, and Poincaré.

I have already referred to the fact that the motion of the planet Mercury cannot be fully accounted for on Newtonian theory. Departures are found in the sense that there appears to be a slow revolution of the orbit as a whole at a rate which is in excess of what can be accounted for on Newtonian theory by 42 seconds of arc per century. It would seem that this is now satisfactorily accounted for in terms of Einstein's theory of general relativity.

There are still many fields of astronomy to which Newton's laws could be profitably applied. The newest of these relates to the motions in the galaxy as a whole and the new branch of dynamics called "stellar dynamics," which is rapidly growing in range and scope. I shall have a few things to say about this later.

Let me turn from this classic example of the universality of nature's laws to a more recent advance which in some ways is as striking. I hardly need point out to an audience in 1946 that the phenomenon of nuclear transformation (more commonly called "atom-smashing") has been studied extensively in recent years. Using the information obtained from such studies, Bethe was able to announce a few years ago that certain nuclear transformations involving carbon and nitrogen can lead indirectly to the synthesis of a helium nucleus from four protons. He was further able to show that, under the conditions for the interior of the sun which had been derived earlier by astrophysicists and with the cross sections for the reactions found in the laboratory, we can account in a most satisfactory way for the source of energy of the sun—a striking example of the synthesis of many types of investigations.

Let me consider one further example. In 1926 Fermi and Dirac were led to a reformulation of the laws of statistical mechanics as they applied to an electron gas and showed that departures from classical laws should be expected at high densities and/or low temperatures. The nature of the departures predicted was this: According to classical laws, the pressure is proportional to the concentration and temperature. If at a given temperature we increase the concentration, then departures set in, in the sense that the pressure begins to increase more rapidly with the concentration and eventually becomes a function of the concentration only. When such a state is reached, one says that the electron gas has become degenerate. These new laws have found extensive applications in the theory of metals and are of the greatest practical importance. But the first application of the new laws was found in an astrophysical context by R. H. Fowler, who used the laws of a Fermi-Dirac gas to elucidate the structure of very dense stars such as the companion of Sirius. These dense stars, commonly known as white dwarfs, have densities of the order of several tons per cubic inch. The most extreme example is a star discovered some years ago by G. P. Kuiper which is estimated to have a density of 620 tons per cubic inch. Fowler immediately recognized that under these conditions the electrons must be degenerate in the sense of the Fermi-Dirac statistics. And with this discovery of Fowler it became possible to work out the constitution of the white dwarf stars.

This subject of the structure of the white dwarf stars has interested me personally, and I may be pardoned if I dwell on it a little longer. An extension of Fowler's discussion soon made it apparent that the laws of Fermi and Dirac required further modifications to take account of the fact that, at the high densities prevailing in the white dwarf stars, there will be a considerable number of electrons moving with velocities comparable to that of light. When modifications resulting from such high velocities are included, it was found that there is an upper limit to the mass of dense stars. This upper limit is in the neighborhood of 1.4 solar masses. The reason for the appearance of this upper limit is that for larger masses no stable equilibrium configuration exists. The recognition of this upper limit raises many questions of interest concerning stellar evolution. And it is not impossible that the occurrence of the supernova phenomenon is in some ways related to this. I shall not go into these matters now, but I mention these only to draw your attention to the manner in which the domain of validity of certain basic laws is continually being extended.

In the three illustrations I have given, I have discussed the applicability of the same laws. But sometimes we have the application of the same set of *ideas* to problems which may appear entirely unrelated at first sight. For example, it is surprising to realize that the same basic ideas which account for the motions of microscopic colloidal particles in solution also account for the motions of stars in clusters. This basic identity of the two problems, which is far-reaching, is one of the most striking phenomena I have personally encountered, and I would like to say a few words about it.

The phenomenon of what is called "Brownian motion" was discovered by the English botanist Brown in 1827, who observed that when small particles (in his case pollen) are suspended in water, then instead of settling down, they get into a state of perpetual agitation. It may be amusing to recall that at first this perpetual motion was thought of as due to the life in the pollen, but Brown soon showed that this cannot be, for even the fine dust gathered from the Sphinx in Egypt exhibited the same behavior! We know now that the Brownian motion arises in consequence of the collisions which the colloidal particles suffer with the molecules of the surrounding fluid. Since even the smallest colloidal particle is several million times more massive than the individual molecules, it is apparent that a single collision can hardly make an impression on the colloidal particle. But the cumulative effect of a large number of collisions can become appreciable, and it is indeed the cause of Brownian motion. It is remarkable that the same methods which have been used to study Brownian motion can also be applied to study the motions of stars in a cluster like the Pleiades. The reason why we can do this is the following: When two stars in a cluster pass each other, the direction and magnitude of the motion of each of the stars change. But on account of the inverse square character of the forces between the stars, each such passage alters the motions only by a very minute amount. And again it is the cumulative effect of a large number of such passages which produces an appreciable change. The analogy with Brownian motion is apparent, and the theory of the motions of stars can be developed along the lines of the theory of Brownian movement. Indeed, the theory in the stellar case gives a more complete picture of Brownian motion than even the motion of colloidal particles provides. I may further mention that the development of this theory enables us to predict in a general way the evolution of star clusters and provides estimates for the time scale of the universe.

PREDICTIONS BASED ON THE BASIC LAWS

I shall now pass on to another aspect of scientific investigations in which predictions are made on the basis of laws derived from other evidence and confirmations are later sought for these same predictions.

I suppose that the most spectacular of such predictions made in recent times, which was later confirmed, is that of Halley. In 1705 Edmund Halley communicated to the Royal Society his memoir on *Astronomiae Cometicae Synopsis*. This classic paper surveys the subject from the earliest times to those of Newton. Next, on Newtonian principles Halley calculated parabolic elements for twenty-four properly observed comets from A.D. 1337 to 1698. It is captivating to turn the pages of this memorable and deeply interesting contribution to knowledge in which no pains are spared for accuracy and completeness. And it is also in this contribution that Halley reflects on the possibility, or rather the probability, that comets move rather in highly elliptical orbits than in parabolic trajectories. In the latter case, comets would come from infinity and go to infinity. However, in the former case, they would be members of the solar system and would be expected to return after a lengthy period of years. It was indeed in view of this probability that Halley undertook the immense computational task, in order that if a new comet should appear we could, on comparing its elements with the computed ones, see whether or not it was an old one returned. He says, further, that many things persuaded him to the belief that the comet of 1531 was the same that was observed in 1607 and that he himself had observed in 1682 and which, moreover, he considered confirmed by one which was roughly observed in 1456. After which he adds: "Whence I would venture to predict with confidence a return of the same *anno scil* in 1758." Such was the origin of Halley's comet, the most celebrated of the comets. It came as predicted, the year after Halley's death, and has appeared on two further occasions since.

A more recent example of such a prediction, which was later confirmed, is that of Dirac concerning the positron. In 1928, by a stroke of singular genius, Dirac wrote down the equation of an electron which predicted a number of things in agreement with experiments. But his equation also predicted that an electron should have states in which it should have negative energy—an unheard-of possibility! However, Dirac was so convinced, on general grounds, of the correctness of his equation that he concluded that these states cannot be denied their reality. To get over the difficulty of all electrons dropping to states of negative energy and producing a bizarre world around us, Dirac suggested that normally all states of negative energy are occupied so that the few remaining electrons with positive energy cannot get into such states, normally speaking, that is. However, he pointed out at the same time that under certain conditions an electron in a state of negative energy could be raised to a state of positive energy, creating in this way an electron and an absence of an electron in the infinite distribution of negative energy. And this *hole* in the distribution of negative energy will behave as though it were a perfectly sensible particle with a positive energy, but with a positive charge. This is the positron, and the phenomenon he had considered is the creation of an electron pair. Dirac even worked out a theory for the probability of such pair creations. Some three years later all these predictions were verified, which confirmed his conviction in the absolute correctness of his equation.

A third and final example I shall consider in this group is Einstein's prediction of the deflection of light in a gravitational field and how it was later confirmed. In telling this story, I shall quote from a lecture by Eddington, who was chiefly responsible for the verification.

The most exciting event I can recall in my own connection with Astronomy is the verification of Einstein's prediction of the deflection of light at the eclipse of 1919. The circumstances were unusual. Plans were begun in 1918 during the war, and it was doubtful until the eleventh hour whether there would be any possibility of the expeditions starting. But it was important not to miss the 1919 eclipse, because it was in an exceptionally good star field: none of the subsequent expeditions have had this advantage. Two expeditions were organized at Greenwich by Sir Frank Dyson, the late Astronomer Royal, the one going to Sobral in Brazil and the other to the isle of Príncipe in West Africa. [Eddington was in charge of the expedition which went to Príncipe.] It was impossible to get any work done by the instrument-makers until after the armistice; and as the expeditions had to sail in February there was a tremendous rush of preparation. The Brazil party had perfect weather for the eclipse; through incidental circumstances their observation could not be reduced until some months later, but in the end they provided the most conclusive confirmation. I was at Príncipe. There the eclipse day came with rain, and cloud-covered sky, which almost took away all hope. Near totality, the sun began to show dimly; and we carried through the program, hoping that the conditions might not be so bad as they seemed. The clouds must have thinned before the end of totality, because amid many failures, we obtained two plates showing the desired star images. These were compared with the plates already taken of the same star field at a time when the sun was elsewhere, so that the difference indicated the apparent displacement of the stars due to the bending of the light rays in passing near the sun.

As the problem then presented itself to us, there were three possibilities. There might be no deflection at all; that is, light might not be subject to gravitation. There might be a "half deflection" signifying that light was subject to gravitation as would follow from Newtonian law. Or there might be a full deflection confirming Einstein's instead of Newton's law. I remember Dyson explaining all this to Cottingham who gathered the main idea, that the bigger the result the more exciting it would be. "What will it mean if we get double the deflection?"

"Then," said Dyson, "Eddington will go mad and you will have to come home alone."

Arrangements had been made to measure the plates on the spot, not merely from impatience, but as a precaution against mishap on the way home; so one of the successful plates was examined immediately. The quantity to be looked for was large as astronomical measures go, so that one plate would virtually decide the question, though confirmation from others would be sought. Three days after the eclipse, as the last lines of the calculation were reached, I knew that Einstein's theory had stood the test and that the new outlook of scientific thought must prevail. Cottingham did not have to go home alone.

IDENTIFICATIONS RESULTING FROM THE BASIC LAWS

I now want to consider a third aspect of scientific investigations which is in a sense intermediate to the kinds I have already described.

During the eighteenth century, the idealist philosopher Bishop Berkeley and his followers claimed that the sun, the moon, and the stars are but "so many sensations in our mind" and that it would be meaningless to inquire, for example, as to the composition of the stars. And yet, only a few decades later, Kirchhoff was to announce in 1860 his momentous chemical interpretation of the Fraunhofer lines showing the presence of the familiar metals as glowing vapors in the sun's atmosphere. From this time onward, to speak of the composition of stars was no longer in the realm of idle dreaming. It became a problem of intense practical interest.

It is hard to believe that, in the eighty years which have followed, the whole problem of the interpretation of the innumerable spectra which have been observed, both in laboratory and in stellar sources, should have reached a stage so near completion. The story of these investigations forms one of the most romantic chapters in the history and methods of science: Indeed, for the most part it cannot be distinguished from the history of physics, chemistry, and astronomy of the last fifty or more years. And if I select from this large field two incidental details for special consideration, it is not because I attach any undue importance or significance to them, but only because I happen to be specially interested in them. What I want to say relates to the two atoms which are, next to hydrogen, the simplest. These are the atoms with two electrons: helium and the negative ion of hydrogen.

First, regarding helium: Until March 1895, helium was known only as a chromospheric element on the sun. It had, in fact, been detected during the total eclipse of the sun which occurred in August 1868 by Jansen, the French astronomer. What Jansen observed was, that in the chromospheric spectrum which appears during the flash at the instant of totality, there is a bright yellow line at λ5876 near the well-known lines of sodium. At first it was thought that this line may also be due to sodium, but it was Sir Norman Lockyer who first realized that this cannot be so and that this new line could not be identified with the lines produced by any of the then-known terrestrial elements. He, therefore, concluded that a new element was involved, and, since it had been detected on the sun, he called it "helium." In 1895, a quarter of a century later, the well-known chemist, Sir William Ramsay, while studying the gases evolved by certain uranium minerals, examined their spectra. He found that in the spectra thus obtained there was a brilliant yellow line exactly at the place of the chromospheric line. Further investigation confirmed that in both cases the same source was involved; and it was thus that the element which had been first detected on the sun was later isolated on the earth.

The story of the negative ion of hydrogen is in some ways equally fascinating. That an atom composed of a proton and two electrons can exist in a free state was established by Bethe and Hylleraas on theoretical grounds. The calculations of Bethe and Hylleraas are such straightforward consequences of the quantum theory that there can be no doubt either of its stability or of its ability to exist in a free state under suitable conditions. But all the same, the fact remains that so far the negative hydrogen-ion had not been isolated as such in the laboratory. However, it was pointed out by Wildt some years ago that negative ions of hydrogen must exist in the free state and in considerable numbers in the atmosphere of the sun. The question arises, "Can we detect it?" In order that we may do this, it is first necessary to know the manner in which the negative ion of hydrogen would absorb light and, further, the effect such an absorption would have on the solar spectrum. The theoretical problem of determining how the negative ion of hydrogen would absorb light turns out to be an exceptionally delicate matter. But the underlying physical problem has now been solved, and it is possible to predict with a fair degree of certainty the effects which may be observed in the solar spectrum. The nature of these effects is so clear cut, and they are so fully borne out by the observations, that it is no exaggeration to say that this atom consisting of a proton and two electrons, which was predicted by the quantum theory to have a stable existence, has now been identified on the sun.

So far I have considered only the sort of things a scientist seeks in the practice of his profession, and I have left to the last the consideration of his motivations. There are several schools of thought here. I reject the view that the motivation springs from a conscious or a subconscious belief that everything he does will eventually find use in the amenities of daily life. I also reject the corollary which insists that a scientist must always consciously integrate his efforts with the social needs and urgencies of his time. But I also do not accept the view that scientists are urged on in their work by a "holy passion" for truth or a "burning curiosity" to unravel the "secrets" of nature. I do not believe that in the daily practice of his profession a scientist has much in common with the Buddha who renounced his princely life to contemplate the ethical and moral values which give meaning and significance to life. And, I am afraid, he has equally little in common with Marco Polo.

What actually does give substance and reality to the efforts of a scientist is his desire to participate actively in the progress of his science to the best of his ability. And if I have to describe in one word what is the prime motive which underlies a scientist's work, I would say *systematization*. That may sound rather prosaic, but I think it approaches the truth. What a scientist tries to do essentially is to select a certain domain, a certain aspect, or a certain detail, and see if that takes its appropriate place in a general scheme which has form and coherence; and, if not, to seek further information which would help him to do that. This is perhaps somewhat vague, particularly, the use of the words "appropriate," "general scheme," "form," and "coherence." I admit that these are things which cannot be defined any more than beauty in art can be defined; but people who are acquainted with the subject have no difficulty in recognizing or appreciating it. Let me try, however, to explain what I mean by considering very briefly two examples.

The phenomenon of radioactivity was discovered by Henri Becquerel in 1896. We know now that there are three radioactive families; that in a radioactive transformation one or more of three distinct types of radiation can be emitted; that the laws of radioactive displacements are involved; that the recognition of the existence of isotopes and isobars is involved; and that a novel theory of spontaneous disintegration of atoms is involved. You can imagine the enormous variety and complexity of the phenomena which radioactivity must have presented to those who did not know any of these things. And yet, when Rutherford's first edition of *Radio-activity* appeared in 1904, the essentials of the phenomenon had already been unraveled. This was largely because the problem had been *systematically* investigated with that energy, orderliness, and thoroughness which are the characteristics of Rutherford.

To take another example: During the period including the First World War and the twenties, the very immense task of unraveling complex atomic spectra was undertaken by the physicists—a task which could not have been completed without conscious efforts toward what I have called "systematization." It was in this way also that the principles of the quantum theory came to be established during the late twenties. And, as the sponsors of this series have expressly asked each contributor to speak from personal experience, I may be permitted to add that the method I have adopted in my own work has always been first to learn what is already known about a subject; then to see if it conforms to those standards of rigor, logical ordering, and completion which one has a right to ask; and, if it does not, to set about doing it. The motivation has always been systematization based on scholarship. And I venture to suppose that this is true quite generally. In any case, it would seem to me that only in that way can a healthy scientific life be led and the real scientific values be achieved.

I am afraid I have left myself no time to discuss a very important phase of scientific work, namely, its cooperative nature. I shall, therefore, content myself with just one quotation from Rutherford:

> It is not in the nature of things for any one man to make a sudden, violent discovery; science goes step by step and every man depends on the work of his predecessors. When you hear of a sudden unexpected discovery—a bolt from the blue, as it were—you can always be sure that it has grown up by the influence of one man on another, and it is the mutual influence which makes the enormous possibility of scientific advance. Scientists are not dependent on the ideas of a single man, but on the combined wisdom of thousands of men, all thinking of the same problem and each doing his little bit to add to the great structure of knowledge which is gradually being erected.

That is the opinion of one of the greatest—I would almost say, the greatest—physicist of our time. You can, therefore, understand why it is that scientists are always internationalists, and why it is that so much apprehension is being expressed by them now at the prospective limitations of the freedom of science.

And, finally, one may ask, "What is the case for the life of a scientist?" The case is this: "that [he has] added something to knowledge, and helped others to add more: and that these somethings have a value which differs in degree only, and not in kind, from that of the creations of the great [scientists], or of any of the other artists, great or small, who have left some kind of memorial behind them" (G. H. Hardy).

2

The Pursuit of Science:
Its Motivations

I

"The Pursuit of Science: Its Motivations" is a difficult subject because of the variety and the range of the motives of the individual scientists; they are as varied as the tastes, the temperaments, and the attitudes of the scientists themselves. Besides, their motivations are subject to substantial changes during the lifetimes of the scientists; indeed, it is difficult to discern a common denominator.

I shall restrict myself to reflections on the lives and the accomplishments of some of the great scientists of the past. Reflecting on the motives and the attitudes of great men is beset with grave semantic difficulties of communication: the words and phrases that language allows have overtones of criticism or judgment. Indeed, when speaking about others, it is well to heed Turgenev's admonition, through his character Insarov, in *On the Eve:*

> We are speaking of other people; why
> bring in yourself?

To set my account in its proper perspective, I shall begin with a conversation between Majorana and Fermi in the mid-1920s when both were also in their middle twenties. The conversation was reported to me by one who was present on the occasion:

This lecture was delivered as the inaugural lecture at the Golden Jubilee Celebrations of the Indian Academy of Sciences in Bangalore on 6 February 1985. It was published in *Current Science* (Bangalore, India) 54 (1985):1–9; and in *Minerva: A Review of Science, Policy, and Learning* 22 (3–4): 410–20, and is reprinted here with permission.

MAJORANA: There are scientists who "happen" only once in every 500 years, like Archimedes or Newton. And there are scientists who happen only once or twice in a century, like Einstein or Bohr.

FERMI: But where do I come in, Majorana?

MAJORANA: Be reasonable, Enrico! I am not talking about you or me. I am talking about Einstein and Bohr.

II

For a discussion of the motivations which impel one to pursue the goals of science, no example is better than that of Johannes Kepler. Kepler's uniqueness derives from the position he occupies at the great crossroads where science shed its enveloping dogmas and the pathway was prepared for Newton. Kepler, in his inquiries, asked questions that none before him, including Copernicus, had asked. Kepler's laws differ qualitatively from earlier assumptions about planetary orbits: the assertion that planetary orbits "are ellipses" in no way resembles the kind of improvements that his predecessors had sought. In his analysis of the motions of the planets, Kepler was not preoccupied with geometrical questions; he asked, instead, questions such as: "What is the origin of planetary motions?" "If the sun is at the center of the solar system, as it is in the Copernican scheme, should not that fact be discernible in the motions and in the orbits of the planets themselves?" These are questions in physics—not in some preconceived geometrical framework.

While Kepler's approach to the problem of planetary motions was radically different from that of anyone before him, his work is preeminent for the manner in which he extracted general laws from a careful examination of observations. His examination was long and it was arduous: it took him twenty and more years of constant and persistent effort, but he never lost sight of his goal. For him, it was a search for the Holy Grail in a very literal sense.

From the outset Kepler realized that a careful study of the orbit of Mars would provide the key to planetary motions because its orbit departs from a circle the most: it had defeated Copernicus; and further that an analysis of the accurate observations of Tycho Brahe was an essential prerequisite. As Kepler wrote:

> Let all keep silence and hark to Tycho who has devoted thirty-five years to his observations. . . . For Tycho alone do I wait; he shall explain to me the order and arrangement of the orbits.[1]

Tycho possesses the best observations, and thus so-to-speak the material for the building of the new edifice.[2]

. . . I believe it was an act of Divine Providence that I arrived just at the time when Longomontanus was occupied with Mars. For Mars alone enables us to penetrate the secrets of astronomy which otherwise would remain forever hidden from us. . .[3]

Indeed, Kepler went to extraordinary lengths to acquire the observations of Tycho which he so badly needed. It is not an exaggeration to say that he committed larceny, for, as he confessed: "I confess that when Tycho died, I quickly took advantage of the absence, or lack of circumspection, of the heirs, by taking the observations under my care, or perhaps usurping them."[4] And as he explained: "The cause of this quarrel lies in the suspicious nature and bad manners of the Brahe family, but on the other hand also in my own passionate and mocking character. It must be admitted that Tengnagel had important reasons for suspecting me. I was in possession of the observations and refused to hand them over to the heirs."[5]

With Tycho's observations thus acquired, Kepler constantly asked himself: "If the sun is indeed the origin and the source of planetary motions, then how does this fact manifest itself in the motions of the planets themselves?" Noticing that Mars moved a little faster when nearest the sun than when farthest away, and "remembering Archimedes," he determined the area described by the radius vector joining the sun to the instantaneous position of Mars, as we follow it in its orbit. As Kepler wrote:

Since I was aware that there exists an infinite number of points on the orbit and accordingly an infinite number of distances [from the sun] the idea occurred to me that the sum of these distances is contained in the *area* of the orbit. For I remembered that in the same manner Archimedes too divided the area of a circle into an infinite number of triangles.[6]

This was how Kepler discovered in July 1603 his law of areas, the second of his three great laws in Newton's enumeration that has been adopted ever since. The establishment of this result took Kepler some five years; for, already prior to the publication of his *Mysterium Cosmographicum* in 1596, he had sought for such a law in connection with his association of the five regular solids with the existence of the six planets known in his time.

The law of areas determined the variation of the speed along its orbit, but it did not determine the shape of the orbit. A year before he had arrived at his final statement of the law of areas, Kepler had in fact discarded circular orbits for the planets, for in October of 1602 he had written: "The conclusion is quite simply that the planet's path is not a circle—it curves inward on both sides and outward again at opposite ends. Such a curve is called an oval. The orbit is not a circle, but an oval figure."[7]

Even after concluding that the orbit of Mars is an "oval," it took Kepler an additional three years to establish that the orbit was in fact an ellipse. When that was established, he wrote:

> Why should I mince my words? The truth of Nature, which I had re-jected and chased away, returned by stealth through the back door, dis-guising itself to be accepted. That is to say, I laid [the original equation] aside, and fell back on ellipses, believing that this was a quite different hypothesis, whereas the two, as I shall prove in the next chapter, are one and the same. . . . I thought and searched, until I went nearly mad, for a reason, why the planet preferred an elliptical orbit [to mine]. . . . Ah, what a foolish bird I have been![8]

Finally, in 1608, his *Astronomia Nova* was published. As Arthur Koestler wrote:

> It was a beautifully printed volume in folio, of which only a few copies survive. The Emperor [Rudolph] claimed the whole edition as his prop-erty and forbade Kepler to sell or give away any copy of it "without our foreknowledge and consent." But since his salary was in arrears, Kepler felt at liberty to do as he liked, and sold the whole edition to the print-ers. Thus the story of the *New Astronomy* begins and ends with acts of larceny, committed *ad majorem Dei gloriam*.[9]

Ten more years elapsed before Kepler discovered his third law: that the squares of the periods of revolution of any two planets is in the ratio of the cubes of their mean distances from the sun. The law is stated in his *Harmonice Mundi* completed in 1618. Here is how Kepler describes his discovery:

> On 8 March of this present year 1618, if precise dates are wanted, [the solution] turned up in my head. But I had an unlucky hand and when I tested it by computations I rejected it as false. In the end it came back to me on 15 May, and in a new attack conquered the darkness of my mind; it agreed so perfectly with the data which my seventeen years of labour on Tycho's observations had yielded, that I thought at first I was dreaming.[10]

Thus ended Kepler's long and arduous search for his Holy Grail.

In his first book, *Mysterium Cosmographicum,* Kepler exclaimed: "Oh! that we could live to see the day when both sets of figures agree with each other."[11] Twenty-two years later, after he had discovered his third law and his poignant cry had been answered, he added the following footnote to this exclamation in a reprinting of *Mysterium Cosmographicum:* "We have lived to see this day after 22 years and rejoice in it, at least I did; I trust that Maestlin and many other men will share in my joy!"[12]

III

In his novel, *The Redemption of Tycho Brahe,* Max Brod—the Czech writer who is also known for publishing, posthumously, the works of Franz Kafka—portrays and contrasts the characters of Tycho Brahe and Kepler. While Brod's novel is grossly inaccurate historically, yet his idea of what a scientist like Kepler might have been is worth quoting:

> Kepler now inspired him [Tycho] with a feeling of awe. The tranquility with which he applied himself to his labours and entirely ignored the warblings of flatterers was to Tycho almost superhuman. There was something incomprehensible in its absence of emotion, like a breath from a distant region of ice . . .[13]

Is the tranquility and the absence of emotion, which Brod attributes to his imagined Kepler, ever attained by a practicing scientist?[14]

IV

The most remarkable aspect of Kepler's pursuit of science is the constancy with which he applied himself to his chosen quest. His "was a character superior in singleness," to use Shelley's phrase. But does the example of Kepler provide any assurance of success for a similar constancy in others? I shall consider two examples.

First, the example of Albert Michelson. His main preoccupation throughout his life was to measure the velocity of light with increasing precision. His interest came about almost by accident, when the commander of the United States Naval Academy asked him—he was then an instructor at the Academy—to prepare some lecture-demonstrations of the velocity of light. That was in 1878, and it led to Michelson's first determination of the velocity of light in 1880. On 7 May 1931, two days before he died and fifty years later, he dictated the opening sentences of a paper, posthumously published, which gave the results of his last measurement. Michelson's efforts resulted in an improvement in our knowledge of the velocity of light from 1 part in 3,000 to 1 part in 30,000, that is, by a factor of 10. But by 1973 the accuracy had been improved to 1 part in 10^{10}, a measurement that made obsolete, beforehand, all future measurements.

Were Michelson's efforts over fifty years in vain? Leaving that question aside, one must record that, during his long career, Michelson made great discoveries derived from his delight in "light waves and their uses." Thus, his development of interferometry, leading to the first direct determination of the diameter of a star, is breathtaking. And who does not know the Michelson–Morley experiment which, through Einstein's formulation of the special and the general theory of relativity, changed irrevocably our understanding of the nature of space and time? It is a curious fact that Michelson himself was never happy with the outcome of his experiment. Indeed, it is recorded that when Einstein visited Michelson in April 1931, Mrs. Michelson felt it necessary to warn Einstein in a whisper when he arrived: "Please don't get him started on the subject of the ether." [15]

A second example is Eddington, who devoted the last sixteen years of his life to developing his "fundamental theory." Of this prodigious effort, he said a year before he died: "At no time during the past 16 years have I felt any doubt about the correctness of my theory." [16] Yet, his efforts have left no trace on subsequent developments.

Is it wise then to pursue science with a single objective and with a singleness of purpose?

V

While Kepler provides the supreme example of sustained scientific effort leading to great and fundamental discoveries, there are instances in which great thoughts have seemingly occurred spontaneously. Thus, Dirac has written that his work on Poisson brackets, and on his relativistic wave equation of the electron, were consequences of ideas "which had just come out of the blue. I could not very well say just how it had occurred to me. And I felt that work of this kind was a rather 'undeserved success.'" [17]

Dirac's recollection, that the ideas underlying his work on Poisson brackets and his relativistic wave equation of the electron came to him "out of the blue," is an example of what is apparently not a unique phenomenon: those who have made great discoveries seem to remember and cherish the occasions on which they made them. Thus, Einstein has recorded that: "When in 1907 I was working on a comprehensive paper on the special theory of relativity . . . there occurred to me the happiest thought of my life . . . that '*for an observer falling freely from the roof of a house there exists*—at least in his immediate surroundings—*no gravitational field.*'" [18] This "happy thought" was, of course, later enshrined in his principle of equivalence that is at the base of his general theory of relativity.

A recollection in a similar vein is that of Fermi. I once had the occasion to ask Fermi, referring to Hadamard's perceptive *Essay on the Psychology of Invention in the Mathematical Field,* what the psychology of invention in the realm of physics might be. Fermi responded by narrating the occasion of his discovery of the effect of slow neutrons on induced radioactivity. This is what he said:

> I will tell you how I came to make the discovery which I suppose is the most important one I have made. We were working very hard on the neutron-induced radioactivity and the results we were obtaining made no sense. One day, as I came to the laboratory, it occurred to me that I should examine the effect of placing a piece of lead before the incident neutrons. Instead of my usual custom, I took great pains to have the piece of lead precisely machined. I was clearly dissatisfied with something; I tried every excuse to postpone putting the piece of lead in its place. When finally, with some reluctance, I was going to put it in place, I said to myself: "No, I do not want this piece of lead here; what I want is a piece of paraffin." It was just like that, with no advance warning, no conscious prior reasoning. I immediately took some odd piece of paraffin and placed it where the piece of lead was to have been.[19]

Perhaps the most moving statement in this general context is that of Heisenberg relating the moment when the laws of quantum mechanics came to a sharp focus in his mind.

> . . . one evening I reached the point where I was ready to determine the individual terms in the energy table, or, as we put it today, in the energy matrix, by what would now be considered an extremely clumsy series of calculations. When the first terms seemed to accord with the energy principle, I became rather excited, and I began to make countless arithmetical errors. As a result, it was almost three o'clock in the morning before the final result of my computations lay before me. The energy principle had held for all terms, and I could no longer doubt the mathematical consistency and coherence of the kind of quantum mechanics to which my calculations pointed. At first, I was deeply alarmed. I had the feeling that, through the surface of atomic phenomena, I was looking at a strangely beautiful interior, and felt almost giddy at the thought that I now had to probe this wealth of mathematical structure nature had so generously spread out before me. I was far too excited to sleep, and so, as a new day dawned, I made for the southern tip of the island, where I had been longing to climb a rock jutting out into the sea. I now did so without too much trouble, and waited for the sun to rise.[20]

There is no difficulty for any of us in sharing in Heisenberg's ex-hilaration of that supreme moment. We all know of the difficulties and paradoxes that beset the "old" Bohr-Sommerfeld quantum theory of the time; and we also know of Heisenberg's long puzzlement with Sommerfeld, Bohr, and Pauli over these difficulties and paradoxes. He had already published at that time his paper with Kramers on the dis-persion theory—a theory which in many ways was the precursor to the developments that were to follow.

But what is our reaction to Heisenberg's account of his ideas on the theory of elementary particles that he developed some thirty years later, after his tragic experiences during the war and his disappoint-ments and frustrations of the post-war years? Mrs. Heisenberg, in her book on her husband, has written: "One moonlight night we walked all over the Hainberg Mountain, and he was completely enthralled by the visions he had, trying to explain his newest discovery to me. He talked about the miracle of symmetry as the original archetype of cre-ation, about harmony, about the beauty of simplicity, and its inner truth."[21] She quotes from one of Heisenberg's letters to her sister at this time:

> In fact, the last few weeks were full of excitement for me. And perhaps I can best illustrate what I have experienced through the analogy that I have attempted an as yet unknown ascent to the fundamental peak of atomic theory, with great efforts during the past five years. And now, with the peak directly ahead of me, the whole terrain of interrelation-ships in atomic theory is suddenly and clearly spread out before my eyes. That these interrelationships display, in all their mathematical ab-straction, an incredible degree of simplicity, is a gift we can only accept humbly. Not even Plato could have believed them to be so beautiful. For these interrelationships cannot be invented; they have been there since the creation of the world.[22]

You will notice the remarkable similarity in language and in phrase-ology with the description of his discovery of the basic rules of quan-tum mechanics some thirty years earlier. But do we share in his second vision in the same way? In the earlier case, his ideas won immediate acceptance. In contrast, his ideas on particle physics were rejected and repudiated even by his long-time critic and friend, Pauli. But it is moving to read what Mrs. Heisenberg writes toward the end of her biography:

> With smiling certainty, he once said to me: "I was lucky enough to look over the good Lord's shoulder while He was at work." That was enough for him, more than enough! It gave him great joy, and the strength to

meet the hostilities and misunderstandings he was subjected to in the world time and again with equanimity, and not to be led astray.[23]

VI

A different aspect of the effect a great discovery can have on its author is provided by Hideki Yukawa, in his autobiography, *The Traveler,* written when Yukawa was past fifty. One would normally have expected that an autobiography entitled *The Traveler* by one whose life, at least as seen from the outside, had been rich and fruitful, would be an account of an entire life. But Yukawa's account of his "travels" ends with the publication of his paper of 1934 describing his great discovery with the sombre note: "I do not want to write beyond this point, because those days when I studied relentlessly are nostalgic to me; and on the other hand, I am sad when I think how I have become increasingly preoccupied with matters other than study."[24]

While all of us can share in the joy of the discoveries of the great men of science, we may be puzzled by what those many, very many, less perceptive and less fortunate are to cherish and remember. Are they, like Vladimir and Estragon in Samuel Beckett's play, destined to wait for Godot? Or are they to console themselves with Milton's thought "they also serve who only stand and wait"?

VII

I now turn to the role of approbation and approval in one's pursuit of science. Wordsworth's example of Newton "voyaging through strange seas of thought alone" is not one that any of us can follow.

I have referred to Eddington's lonely efforts in pursuing his fundamental theory. In spite of the confidence he expressed in the correctness of his theory, Eddington must have been deeply frustrated by the neglect of his work by contemporaries. This frustration is evident in his plaintive letter to Dingle written a few months before he died:

> I am continually trying to find out why people find the procedure obscure. But I would point out that even Einstein was considered obscure, and hundreds of people have thought it necessary to explain him. I cannot seriously believe that I ever attain the obscurity that Dirac does. But in the case of Einstein and Dirac people have thought it worthwhile to penetrate the obscurity. I believe they will understand me all right when they realize they have got to do so—and when it becomes the fashion "to explain Eddington."[25]

The lack of approval by one's contemporaries can have tragic consequences when it is expressed in the form of sharp and violent criticism. Thus, Ludwig Boltzmann, greatly depressed by the violence of the attacks directed against his ideas by Ostwald and Mach, committed suicide, "a martyr to his ideas," as his grandson Flamm has written. And Georg Cantor, the originator of the modern theory of sets of points and of the orders of infinity, lost his mind because of the hatred and the animosity against him and his ideas by his teacher Leopold Kronecker: he was confined to a mental hospital for many years at the end of his life.

VIII

A case very different from the ones I have considered so far is that of Rutherford.

Consider his record. In 1897 he analyzed radioactive radiations into α-particles, β-rays, and γ-rays in a nomenclature he then introduced. In 1902 he formulated the laws of radioactive disintegration—the first time a physical law was formulated in terms of probability and not certainty, and a forerunner of the probability interpretation of quantum mechanics that was to become universal some twenty-five years later. Between 1905 and 1907 he formulated, with Soddy, the laws of radioactive displacement and identified the α-particle as the nucleus of the helium atom; and, with Boltwood, he initiated the determination of the ages of rocks and minerals by their radioactivity. In 1909–10, there were the experiments of Geiger and Marsden, the discovery of the large-angle scattering of α-rays, and Rutherford's formulation of the law of scattering and the nuclear model of the atom. Then in 1917 he effected the first laboratory transformation of atoms: that of nitrogen-14 into oxygen-17 and a proton by α-ray bombardment. In the 1920s he was associated with the clarification of the relationship between the α-ray and the γ-ray spectra. And 1932—the *annus mirabilis,* as R. H. Fowler called it—saw the discovery of the artificial disintegration of lithium-7 into two α-particles by Cockcroft and Walton, of positrons in cosmic-ray showers by Blackett, and of the neutron by Chadwick—all of them in Rutherford's Cavendish Laboratory at Cambridge. In the following year, with Oliphant, Rutherford himself discovered hydrogen-3 and helium-3.

Rutherford's attitude to his own discoveries is illustrated by his response to a remark of someone present at the moment of one of his great discoveries: "Rutherford, you are always on the crest of the wave." Rutherford responded: "I made the wave, didn't I?" Somehow from Rutherford's vantage point everything he said seems right, even including his remark, "I do not let my boys waste their time," when asked if he encouraged his students to study relativity. Rutherford was a happy warrior if ever there was one.

IX

So far, I have tried to illustrate facets of the pursuit of science by drawing on incidents in the lives of some great men of science. I return now to some more general matters, and start with an example. When Michelson was asked, towards the end of his life, why he had devoted such a large fraction of his time to the measurement of the velocity of light, he is said to have replied, "It was so much fun." There is no denying that "fun" does play a role in the pursuit of science. But the word "fun" suggests a lack of seriousness. Indeed, *The Concise Oxford Dictionary* gives to "fun" the meaning "drollery." We can be certain that Michelson did not have that meaning in mind when he described his life's main interest as "fun." What, then, is the precise meaning we are to attach to "fun" in the context in which Michelson used it? More generally, what is the role of pleasure and enjoyment?

While "pleasure" and "enjoyment" are often used to characterize one's efforts in science, failures, frustrations, and disappointments are equally, if not the more, common ingredients of scientific experience. Overcoming difficulties, undoubtedly, contributes to one's final enjoyment of success. Is failure, then, a purely negative aspect of the pursuit of science?

A remark by Dirac describing the rapid development of physics following the founding of the principles of quantum mechanics in the middle and the late 1920s is apposite in this connection:

> It was a good description to say that it was a game, a very interesting game one could play. Whenever one solved one of the little problems, one could write a paper about it. It was very easy in those days for any second-rate physicist to do first-rate work. There has not been such a glorious time since then.[26]

Consider in the context of these remarks, J. J. Thomson's assessment of Lord Rayleigh in his memorial address given in Westminster Abbey:

> There are some great men of science whose charm consists in having said the first word on a subject, in having introduced some new idea which has proved fruitful; there are others whose charm consists perhaps in having said the last word on the subject, and who have reduced

the subject to logical consistency and clearness. I think by temperament Lord Rayleigh belonged to the second group.[27]

This assessment by J. J. Thomson has sometimes been described as double-edged. But could one not conclude, instead, that Rayleigh by temperament chose to address himself to difficult problems and was not content to play the kind of games that Dirac describes in his characterization of the "glorious time" in physics as a time "when second-rate physicists could do first-rate work"?

This last question concerning Rayleigh's temperament raises the further question: after a scientist has reached maturity, what are the reasons for his continued pursuit of science? To what extent are they personal? To what extent are aesthetic criteria, like the perception of order and pattern, form and substance, relevant? Are such aesthetic and personal criteria exclusive? Has a sense of obligation a role? I do not mean obligation with the common meaning of obligation to one's students, one's colleagues, and one's community. I mean, rather, obligation to science itself. And what, indeed, is the content of obligation in the pursuit of science *for* science?

Let me finally turn to a different aspect. G. H. Hardy concludes *A Mathematician's Apology* with the following statement:

> The case for my life, then, or for that of anyone else who has been a mathematician in the same sense in which I have been one, is this: that I have added something to knowledge, and helped others to add more: and that these somethings have a value which differs in degree only, and not in kind, from that of the creations of the great mathematicians, or of any of the other artists, great or small, who have left some kind of memorial behind them.[28]

Hardy's statement referred to mathematicians; but it is equally applicable to all scientists. I want to draw your attention particularly to his reference to wanting to leave behind some kind of memorial, that is, something that posterity may judge. To what extent, then, is the judgment of posterity—which one can never know—a conscious motivation in the pursuit of science?

X

The pursuit of science has often been compared to the scaling of mountains, high and not so high. But who amongst us can hope, even in imagination, to scale the Everest and reach its summit when the sky is blue and the air is still, and in the stillness of the air survey the entire Himalayan range in the dazzling white of the snow stretching to infinity? None of us can hope for a comparable vision of nature and of the universe around us. But there is nothing mean or lowly in standing in the valley below and awaiting the sun to rise over Kinchinjunga.

NOTES

1. Letter to Maestlin, 16–26 February 1599, in *Johannes Kepler gesammelte Werke,* ed. W. von Dyck and M. Caspar (Munich, 1938), 13:289 (hereinafter cited as *Gesammelte Werke*). Quoted in Arthur Koestler, *The Sleepwalkers* (London: Hutchinson, 1959), p. 278.

2. Letter to Herwart, 12 July 1600, *Gesammelte Werke* 14:218 (Koestler, p. 104).

3. Kepler, *Astronomia nova,* in *Gesammelte Werke,* vol. 3, dedication (Koestler, p. 325).

4. Letter to Heyden, October 1605, *Gesammelte Werke* 15:231 (Koestler, p. 345).

5. Letter to D. Fabricius, 1 October 1602, *Gesammelte Werke* 15:17 (Koestler, p. 345).

6. Kepler, *Astronomia nova,* chap. 40 (Koestler, p. 327).

7. Kepler, *Astronomia nova,* chap. 44 (Koestler, p. 329).

8. *Gesammelte Werke* 15:314 (Koestler, p. 333).

9. Koestler, p. 340.

10. *Gesammelte Werke* 16:373 (Koestler, pp. 394–95).

11. *Gesammelte Werke,* vol. 1, chap. 21 (Koestler, p. 260).

12. Ibid., note 7.

13. Max Brod, *The Redemption of Tycho Brahe* (New York: Knopf, 1928), p. 157.

14. When he wrote *The Redemption of Tycho Brahe,* Max Brod was a member of the small circle in Prague that included Einstein and Franz Kafka. Brod's portrayal of Kepler is said to have been influenced by his association with Einstein. Thus, Walter Nernst is reported to have said to Einstein: "You are this man Kepler." See Philip Frank, *Einstein: His Life and Times* (New York: Knopf, 1947), p. 85.

15. Dorothy Michelson Livingston, *The Master of Light: A Biography of Albert A. Michelson* (Chicago: University of Chicago Press, 1974), p. 334.

16. A. Eddington, Dublin Institute of Advanced Studies A, 1943, p. 1.

17. P. A. M. Dirac, "Recollections of an Exciting Era." in *History of Twentieth Century Physics,* Proceedings of the International School of Physics, "Enrico Fermi" (New York: Academic Press, 1977), pp. 137–38.

18. A. Pais, *Subtle is the Lord* (New York: Oxford University Press, 1982), p. 178.

19. S. Chandrasekhar, *Enrico Fermi: Collected Papers,* 2 vols. (Chicago: University of Chicago Press, 1962), 2:926–27.

20. W. Heisenberg, *Physics and Beyond: Encounters and Conversations* (New York: Harper & Row, 1971), p. 61.

21. E. Heisenberg, *Inner Exile,* trans. S. Cappellari and C. Morris (Boston: Birkhäuser, 1984), p. 143.

22. Ibid., pp. 143–44.

23. Ibid., p. 157.

24. H. Yukawa, *Tabibito* (*The Traveler*) (Singapore: World Scientific Publishing, 1982), p. 207.

25. J. G. Crowther, *British Scientists of the Twentieth Century* (London: Routledge & Kegan Paul, 1952), p. 194.

26. P. A. M. Dirac, *Directions in Physics* (New York: Wiley, 1978), p. 7.

27. R. J. Strutt, 4th Baron Rayleigh, *Life of John William Strutt, Third Baron Rayleigh, O.M., F.R.S.* (Madison: University of Wisconsin Press, 1968), p. 310.

28. G. H. Hardy, *A Mathematician's Apology* (Cambridge: Cambridge University Press, 1967), p. 151.

3

THE NORA AND EDWARD RYERSON LECTURE
Shakespeare, Newton, and Beethoven, or Patterns of Creativity

Prefacing a somewhat derogatory criticism of Milton, T. S. Eliot once stated that "the only jury of judgement" that he would accept on his views was that "of the ablest poetical practitioners of his time." Ten years later, perhaps in a more mellow mood, he added: "the scholar and the practitioner, in the field of literary criticism, should supplement each others' work. The criticism of the practitioner will be all the better, certainly, if he is not wholly destitute of scholarship; and the criticism of the scholar will be all the better if he has some experience of the difficulties of writing verse." By the same criterion, anyone who is emboldened to ask if there are discernible differences in the patterns of creativity among the practitioners in the arts and the practitioners in the sciences, must be a practitioner, as well as a scholar, in the arts as well as in the sciences. It will not suffice to be a practitioner in the arts only, or in the sciences only. Certainly, a wanderer, often lonely, in some of the by-lanes of the physical sciences, has simply not the circumference of comprehension to address himself to a question which encompasses the arts and the sciences. I, therefore, begin by asking your forbearance.

Allowing, as we must, for the innumerable individual differences in tastes, temperaments, and comprehension, we ask: Can we in fact discern any major differences in the patterns of creativity among the practitioners in the arts and the practitioners in the sciences? The way I propose to approach this question is to examine, first, the creative

This was the second Nora and Edward Ryerson Lecture delivered at the University of Chicago, Center for Public Policy, on 22 April 1975. It was later published by the Center for Public Policy, and is reprinted here with permission.

patterns of Shakespeare, Newton, and Beethoven, who, by common consent, have, each in his own way, scaled the very summits of human achievement. I shall then seek to determine whether, from the likenesses and the differences in the patterns at these rarified heights, we can draw any larger conclusions which may be valid at lower levels.

I

I begin with Shakespeare.

Shakespeare's education was simple, as Elizabethan education was. While it sufficed and stood him in good stead, Shakespeare was never persuaded by scholarship as such. He clearly expressed his attitude in

> Small have continual plodders ever won
> Save base authority from others' books.

or

> Oh, this learning, what a thing it is!

Even so, when Shakespeare arrived in London in 1587, at the age of twenty-three, he had none of the advantages of a London background that Lodge and Kyd had, or the advantages of years at Oxford or Cambridge that Peele, Lyly, Greene, Marlowe, and Nashe had. There can be little doubt that Shakespeare was acutely aware of his shortcomings and his handicaps. He overcame them by reading and absorbing whatever came his way. The publication of the revised second edition of Holinshed's *Chronicles of England, Scotland, and Ireland,* was particularly timely: it provided Shakespeare with the inspiration for his chronicle plays yet to come.

By 1592, Shakespeare had written his three parts of *Henry VI* and his early comedies, *The Comedy of Errors, Love's Labour's Lost,* and *Two Gentlemen of Verona.* His success with these plays produced Robert Greene's vicious attack on him in that year. Greene was six years older than Shakespeare, and he was among the most prominent figures in the literary life of London at that time. As it happened, Greene's attack was posthumous, as he had died somewhat earlier as the result of a fatal banquet, it is said, "of Rhenish wine and pickled herrings." It was therefore "a time bomb which Greene left." His attack in part read:

> For there is an upstart crow, beautified by our feathers, that with his "Tiger's heart wrapped in a player's hide," supposes he is as well able to bombast out a blank verse as the best of you, and being an absolute Johannes Factotum, is in his own conceit the only Shake-scene in a country.

Greene's attack brings out very clearly that Shakespeare was considered an outsider and an intruder: he had no university background and he did not belong to the aristocratic court circles.

In spite of his early successes, life for Shakespeare, as a player and a playwright, was fraught with uncertainties with the recurring years of the plague and the periodic closing of the theaters in London. But in 1590, Shakespeare found a patron, a friend, and love.

Shakespeare's patron was the young Earl of Southampton who came of age in 1591. The intensity of Shakespeare's emotional experience in the four years that followed was decisive for the development of his art and for the opportunities that opened up for him. Shakespeare's genius matured and flowered with an unexampled outburst of creative activity. Besides the plays already mentioned, he wrote *The Merchant of Venice, The Taming of the Shrew,* and *Richard III.* The two splendid narrative poems, *Venus and Adonis* and *The Rape of Lucrece,* dedicated to the Earl of Southampton, belong to this same period.

During 1592–95, Shakespeare wrote his sonnets as a part of his services for Southampton's patronage. The sonnets are the most autobiographical ever written. They throw a flood of light on Shakespeare's attitude to himself and his art; and they also reveal the extent of his dependence on Southampton's friendship and patronage.

The course of the friendship between Southampton and Shakespeare was by no means smooth. There was the difference in their ages; there was the disparity in their stations, as the aristocratic patron and a player poet; and besides, there was the complication of Shakespeare's mistress—the dark lady of the sonnets—turning her attention away from Shakespeare to the responsive Earl. Shakespeare poured his feelings with poignant sincerity into the sonnets:

When, in disgrace with fortune and men's eyes,
I all alone beweep my outcast state,
And trouble deaf heaven with my bootless cries,
And look upon myself and curse my fate: (29)

Against that time, if ever that time come,
When I shall see thee frown on my defects,
When as thy love hath cast his utmost sum,
Called to that audit by advised respects;
Against that time when thou shalt strangely pass,
And scarcely greet me with that sun, thine eye,
When love, converted from the thing it was,
Shall reasons find for that settled gravity:
Against that time do I ensconce me here

Within the knowledge of mine own desert,
And this my hand against myself uprear,
To guard the lawful reasons on thy part:
> To leave poor me thou hast the strength of laws,
> Since why to love I can allege no cause. (49)

Their relationship, at least as perceived by Shakespeare, was so fragile
that he even considers the possibility of death:

No longer mourn for me when I am dead
Than you shall hear the surly sullen bell
Give warning to the world that I am fled
From this vile world with vilest worms to dwell. (71)

And Shakespeare feels that his life cannot last longer than Southampton's love and that it will come to an end with it.

But do thy worst to steal thyself away,
For term of life thou art assurèd mine;
And life no longer than thy love will stay,
For it depends upon that love of thine.
Then need I not to fear the worst of wrongs,
When in the least of them my life hath end;
I see a better state to me belongs
Than that which on thy humour doth depend.
Thou canst not vex me with inconstant mind,
Since that my life on thy revolt doth lie.
O, what a happy title do I find,
Happy to have thy love, happy to die!
> But what's so blessed-fair that fears no blot?
> Thou mayst be false, and yet I know it not. (92)

In spite of the uncertainty which pervades the entire sonnet sequence, Shakespeare's prophetic confidence in his own poetry occasionally erupts. Thus, in the famous sonnet 55, we have the outpouring:

Not marble, nor the gilded monuments
Of princes, shall outlive this powerful rhyme;
But you shall shine more bright in these contents
Than unswept stone, besmeared with sluttish time.
When wasteful war shall statues overturn,
And broils root out the work of masonry,
Nor Mars's sword nor war's quick fire shall burn,
The living record of your memory.

Meantime, Marlowe appears as a dangerous rival to Southampton's patronage. To offset Shakespeare's *Venus and Adonis,* Marlowe began writing his *Hero and Leander.* Shakespeare expresses his uneasiness with this rivalry while conceding Marlowe's superiority:

> O, how I faint when I of you do write,
> Knowing a better spirit doth use your name,
> And in the praise thereof spends all his might,
> To make me tongue-tied speaking of your fame!
> But since your worth, wide as the ocean is,
> The humble, as the proudest sail doth bear,
> My saucy bark, inferior far to his,
> On your broad main doth willfully appear.
> Your shallowest help will hold me up afloat,
> Whilst he upon your soundless depth doth ride;
> Or, being wrecked, I am a worthless boat,
> He of tall building and of goodly pride.
>   Then if he thrive and I be cast away
>   The worst was this: my love was my decay. (80)

Marlowe died in 1593 in an unhappy brawl which Shakespeare clearly had in mind when he made Touchstone, in *As You Like It,* say:

> When a man's verses cannot be understood, nor a man's good wit sec-
> onded with the forward child Understanding, it strikes a man more
> dead than a great reckoning in a little room.

In the same play, Shakespeare also paid Marlowe the unusual tribute of addressing him as "Dead shepherd" and quoting his line:

> Who ever loved that loved not at first sight?

And before long, the unhappy episode with the "dark lady" also ended:

>   I am perjured most
> For all my vows are oaths to misuse thee,
> And all my honest faith in thee is lost. (152)

With the last sonnet of the Southampton sequence, Shakespeare emerges triumphant:

> No, let me be obsequious in thy heart,
> And take thou my oblation, poor but free,
> Which is not mixed with seconds, knows no art
> But mutual render, only me for thee. (125)

Yes! "poor but free," "not mixed with seconds," and "only me for thee."

In 1594, the Earl of Southampton gave Shakespeare some such amount as £100 to acquire a share in Lord Chamberlain's company when it was formed. With the future thus assured, Shakespeare's natural spirits rose and his genius matured. *A Midsummer Night's Dream,* which he wrote in that year, was the first of his great masterpieces. Soon *Romeo and Juliet, As You Like It,* and *Much Ado About Nothing* followed. Then Shakespeare turned again to his chronicle plays: *King John,* the two parts of *Henry IV,* and *Henry V.* The one hero in all these chronicle plays is England; and in them Shakespeare gives lasting expression to "the very age and body of the time."

Many consider the two parts of *Henry IV* as the twin summits of Shakespeare's achievement in his chronicle plays. They are certainly superlative plays made more memorable by the character of Falstaff. It has been said that "in a totally different way, Falstaff is to English literature what his contemporary Don Quixote has been to the Spanish."

The great "middle period" of Shakespeare begins with *A Midsummer Night's Dream* and ends with *Hamlet* (1600–1601).

In *Hamlet* Shakespeare gives expression to his thoughts on the theater and also his reaction to the rising rivalry with Ben Jonson and the Blackfriar's theater with their appeal to wit and fashion. Thus, in his instruction to the players (in the play within the play), we find Hamlet saying:

> For anything so overdone is from the purpose of playing, whose end, both at the first and now, was and is to hold, as 'twere, the mirror up to nature, to show virtue her own feature, scorn her own image, and the very age and body of the time his form and pressure.

Shakespeare is here asserting that "the very age and body of the time" can be expressed in drama—as, indeed, he had expressed his own age in his chronicle plays.

There is perhaps a hint of admonition to Ben Jonson and the "reformers" in

> O it offends me to the soul to hear a robustious periwig-pated fellow tear a passion to tatters, to very rags, to split the ears of the groundlings, who for the most part, are capable of nothing but inexplicable dumb-shows and noise:

O there be players that I have seen play and heard others praise . . . have so strutted and bellowed that I have thought some of nature's journey-men had made men, and not made them well, they imitated humanity so abominably.

. . .

O reform it altogether.

The plays that followed *Hamlet*—*All's Well That Ends Well* and *Measure for Measure*—provide indications that, at this time, Shakespeare's "nerves were on edge": he appears disillusioned with men and things—perhaps, a proper frame of mind to embark on his great trage-dies. As A. L. Rowse, the distinguished Elizabethan and Shakespearian scholar, has written, the great tragedies "show evidences of strain and exhaustion"; he continues:

As in all significant work, we have a convergence of factors, on the one side literary, on the other personal . . . If Shakespeare were to compare with his rival Ben Jonson he must do so now in tragedy. With the trage-dies he was to make the grandest efforts, extend his powers to his fullest capacity and thus fulfill his destiny as a writer . . . There is cumulative evidence that so far from not caring about his fame and achievement as a writer, his ambition was the highest. The argument has come full circle: here is a personal consideration.

When Shakespeare's work was complete, Ben Jonson was able to com-pare him only with the great tragedians: Aeschylus, Sophocles, and Euripides.

The years 1604–08 saw in succession the plays *Othello*, *King Lear*, *Macbeth*, *Antony and Cleopatra*, and *Coriolanus*. It staggers one's imagi-nation to realize that these great plays, so utterly different from one another, could have been written, in succession, with such unfaltering inspiration.

Here is Hazlitt's summing up of the tragedies:

Macbeth and *Lear*, *Othello* and *Hamlet*, are usually reckoned Shake-speare's four principal tragedies. *Lear* stands first for the profound in-tensity of the passion; *Macbeth* for the wildness of the imagination and the rapidity of action; *Othello* for the progressive interest and powerful alternations of feeling; *Hamlet* for the refined development of thought and sentiment. If the force of genius shown in each of these works is astonishing, their variety is not less so. They are like different creations of the same mind, not one of which has the slightest reference to the rest. This distinctness and originality is indeed the necessary consequences of truth and nature.

Hazlitt does not include *Antony and Cleopatra* among the great tragedies. But nowadays it is considered by many as equally great. As T. S. Eliot in a remarkably sensitive analysis of *Antony and Cleopatra* has said:

> This is a play for mature actors and for a mature audience, for neither on the stage nor in the audience can immature people enter into the feelings of these middle-aged lovers . . . The peculiar triumph of *Antony and Cleopatra* is in the fusion of the heroic and the sordid, in the same characters in one vision of life. Marlowe could have made them seem equally majestic. Dryden in his later play on the subject almost does so. But only Shakespeare could have made them at once majestic and human in their weakness; and without the human weaknesses we should not have the greatness and the terror of tragedy. And the reason is that Shakespeare had learned to say things in poetry which no one else could have said in prose.

It has sometimes been suggested that the plays which followed the great tragedies—*Timon of Athens, Pericles, Prince of Tyre,* and *Cymbeline*—all show signs of nervous fatigue. As A. L. Rowse has remarked: "there seems to be a hiatus here, a pause, if not something more, during these years." But a contrary view has been expressed by T. S. Eliot:

> The last plays are more difficult. Our astonishment in reading and hearing *Antony and Cleopatra* might often in many places be expressed by the words, "I should never have thought that that would be said in poetry." Our moments of astonishment in the later plays could better be expressed by the words, "I should never have thought that that could be said at all." For in the last plays, and I mean especially *Cymbeline, The Winter's Tale, Pericles,* and *The Tempest,* Shakespeare has abandoned the realism of ordinary existence in order to reveal to us a further world of emotion . . .

In any event, Shakespeare's last three plays—*The Winter's Tale, The Tempest,* and *Henry VIII*—are more accessible—at least, Shakespeare's natural poise is more evident. Thus, *Winter's Tale* is a most beautiful and moving play. Hazlitt describes it as "one of the best acting of our author's plays," while the well-known Shakespearian scholar Q. writes: "*Winter's Tale* is beyond criticism and even beyond praise."

In his penultimate play, Shakespeare, ever searching for something new, deals with a profound theme which continues to be vexatious down to this day: in his creation of Caliban, he concretely states for us a central issue of the present age. But the mood of *The Tempest* is one of farewell:

> Our revels are now ended. These our actors,
>> As I foretold you, were all spirits, and
>> Are melted into air, into thin air:
>> And like the baseless fabric of this vision,
>> The cloud-capped towers, the gorgeous palaces,
>> The solemn temples, the great globe itself,
>> Yea, all which it inherit, shall dissolve,
>> And, like this insubstantial pageant faded,
>> Leave not a rack behind.

And finally, in his last play, Shakespeare returns to his chronicle of the English story, which he began with *Henry VI* and *Richard III,* and completes the cycle with *Henry VIII* and the birth of Elizabeth. The concluding speech by the Archbishop of Canterbury opening with the incantation:

> This royal infant—Heaven still move about her—
>> Though in her cradle, yet now promises
>> Upon this land a thousand thousand blessings,

is a form of prophesy of what the Elizabethan age was to be. It gave Shakespeare the splendid opportunity to pay his tribute to the Queen, he had not eulogized at her death in 1603, and to sum up the Elizabethan age now only an imprint on time. As A. L. Rowse concludes his biography of Shakespeare:

> And this too was Shakespeare's end. But like a splendid coiled snake, glittering and richly iridescent—emblem alike of wisdom and immortality—his work lay about him rounded and complete.

Ben Jonson's tribute, included with the first folio, has been prophetic:

> He was not of an age, but of all time!

Let me conclude by quoting two contemporary writers.

Virginia Woolf, after a vain effort imagining how Shakespeare "coined his words," writes in her diary:

> Indeed, I could say that Shakespeare surpasses literature altogether, if I knew what it meant.

And T. S. Eliot sums up Shakespeare as follows:

> The standard set by Shakespeare is that of continuous development from first to last, a development in which the choice both of theme and

of dramatic and verse technique in each play seems to be determined increasingly by Shakespeare's state of feeling by the particular stage of his emotional maturity at the time . . . We may say confidently that the full meaning of any one of his plays is not in itself alone, but in that play in the order in which it was written, in its relation to all of Shakespeare's other plays, earlier and later: we must know all of Shakespeare's work in order to know any of it. No other dramatist of the time approaches anywhere near to this perfection of pattern . . .

It seems to me to correspond to some law of nature that the work of a man like Shakespeare, whose development in the course of his career was so amazing, that it should reach, as in *Hamlet,* the point at which it can touch the imagination and feeling of the maximum number of people to the greatest possible depth and that, thereafter, like a comet which has approached the earth and then continued away on its course, he should gradually recede from view until he tends to disappear into his private mystery.

II

I now turn to Beethoven with more qualms: I am even more painfully aware of my shortcomings to discourse on him.

When Beethoven came to Vienna in 1792, at the age of twenty-two, his attitude must have been one of caution: his studies with Haydn, Schenk, Albrechtsberger, and Salieri were, we may assume, primarily for finding out if there were things he could learn from them. He clearly absorbed what they had to teach him without distorting his own musical ideas. In any event, once he found that he could over-power everyone in Vienna by the sheer virtuosity of his improvisations on the pianoforte, he became impatient and, sometimes, even defiant. Thus, Haydn's unfavorable opinion of the third of his three trios, Opus 1, only confirmed Beethoven's own opinion that it was the best of the three and that Haydn's contrary view was due to jealousy and malice.

At this time, Beethoven desired great fame; and he seems to have been convinced that his sheer strength was sufficient to protect him against all misfortune. This attitude is clearly expressed in his letter to von Zmeskall:

The devil take you! I do not know anything about your whole system of ethics. Power is the morality of men who stand out from the rest, and it is also mine.

This supreme confidence in himself, derived from this morality of power, was soon destined to be tried most sorely.

The first signs of his deafness appeared, already, when Beethoven was twenty-eight years. His initial reaction was one of rage at what he considered as the senselessness of the affliction. As he wrote to Karl Amenda three years later (1801):

Your Beethoven is most unhappy and at strife with nature and Creator. I have often cursed the latter for exposing his creatures to the merest accident, so that often the most beautiful buds are broken or destroyed thereby. Only think that my noblest faculty, my hearing, has greatly deteriorated.

But his fortitude was unshaken, for he continued:

I am resolved to rise superior to every obstacle . . . I am sure my fortune will not desert me. With whom need I be afraid of measuring my strength . . . I will take Fate by the throat.

We obtain a proper appreciation of the state of Beethoven's mind at this time from his famous Heiligenstadt testament written in 1802 but discovered among his papers only after his death. The Heiligenstadt testament is so transparently sincere that it should really be read in its entirety, but the following extract must suffice:

But how humiliated I have felt if somebody standing beside me heard the sound of a flute in the distance and I heard nothing, or if somebody heard a shepherd sing and again I heard nothing—Such experiences almost made me despair, and I was on the point of putting an end to my life—The only thing that held me back was my art. For indeed it seemed impossible to leave this world before I had produced all the works that I felt urged to compose.

Beethoven's confession that he contemplated suicide and that it was the power of his unfulfilled art that saved him finds an echo in what he wrote twenty years later:

I live only for my art and to fulfill my duties as a man.

It is clear that Beethoven's growing deafness shattered his earlier ethics of the morality of power. But like a phoenix it rose only to sustain the realization of his creative powers. Thus, by the time (1807) he came to writing his third Rasoumowsky quartet, his resignation to his affliction appears to be complete, for we find him writing in the margin:

Let your deafness no longer be secret even for art . . .

And the work on the grand scale in which his conflict with fate is taken for granted and ignored is his seventh symphony.

This "middle period" of intense creativeness lasted for some ten years. By his early forties, Beethoven had composed his eight symphonies, his five piano concertos, his one violin concerto, his twenty-five piano sonatas, his eleven quartets, his seven overtures, his one opera, and his one mass. At the age of forty-two with this magnificent pile of compositions behind him, Beethoven practically stopped composing for the next seven years. The fruits of his meditation—so they must have been—came after this period of quiescence in a manner that is perhaps without parallel in musical history.

From the first symphony written in 1801 to the eighth symphony written in 1812, it is essentially the same Beethoven: it is, in fact, the Beethoven of the common understanding. But the Beethoven of the ninth symphony, of the mass in D, of the last four piano sonatas, and, most of all, the last five quartets is an altogether different Beethoven. Beethoven's own pupil, Czerny, did not understand his music of this last period, and he tried to explain it away as due to Beethoven's deafness:

> Beethoven's third style dates from the time when he became gradually completely deaf . . . Thence comes the dissimilarity of the style of his last three sonatas . . . Thence many harmonic roughnesses . . .

By all accounts, Beethoven's last quartets are a Mount Everest of an achievement. Here is a sample of what has been said about them:

> They are peerless.
> They are beyond description or analysis in words.
> The last quartets are unique, unique for Beethoven, unique in all music.

But this much may certainly be said: Nobody can say what the quartets really mean; we can only be sure that they express ideas nowhere else to be found. Wordsworth's description of Newton's mind "as voyaging through strange seas of thought alone" applies equally to Beethoven's mind of this last period.

Beethoven's last complete work, the quartet No. 16 in F major, provides a noble ending to his great sequence. Of this quartet, J. W. N. Sullivan has written:

> It is the work of a man who is fundamentally at peace. It is the peace of a man who has known conflicts, but whose conflicts are now reminiscent. This quality is most apparent in the last movement with its motto, "*Muss es sein? Es muss sein!*" (Must it be? It must be!)

Reviewing the life and work of Beethoven, Sullivan sums him up as follows:

One of the most significant facts, for the understanding of Beethoven, is that his work shows an organic development up until the very end . . . The greatest music Beethoven ever wrote is to be found in the last string quartets, and the music of every decade before the final period was greater than its predecessor.

It is striking how close this summing of Beethoven is to T. S. Eliot's summing of Shakespeare which I quoted earlier. The way Shakespeare and Beethoven overcame the crises of their early years, the continual growth of their minds, the organic unity of their works spanning their entire lives, their great masterpieces towards the end, and even the moods of farewell in *The Tempest* and in the sixteenth quartet, all these are indeed most striking.

III

I now turn to Newton.

Isaac Newton, a posthumous child, born with no father on Christmas Day 1642, was, as Maynard Keynes has aptly written, "the last wonder child to whom the Magi could do sincere and appropriate homage."

One of the most remarkable aspects of Newton's most remarkable life is the explosive outburst of his genius. He was not an infant prodigy; and it is probable that when he went to Cambridge in 1661, he knew little more than elementary arithmetic. And it must be remembered that the new outlook on scientific thought that we associate with the names of Galileo, Kepler, and Descartes had hardly yet penetrated the walls of Oxford and Cambridge. Nevertheless, by 1664, when Newton was in his twenty-third year, his genius seems to have flowered. Thus, Newton recalled in his old age that he had "found the method of Infinite Series at such time (1664–65)." Newton, in fact, wrote out his notes as a connected essay entitled, "On Analysis of Equations with an Infinite Number of Terms" and allowed Barrow to send it to Collins, stipulating, however, that he remain anonymous. This stipulation was withdrawn later; but we encounter here the first indication of a trait which was later to become an obsession with Newton.

By the summer of 1665, when Cambridge was evacuated on account of the plague and Newton had gone to Woolsthorpe, his genius was fully in flower. It manifested itself in a manner unsurpassed in the history of scientific thought. But it was not until many years later that the world was to know what happened during the two years that Newton was at Woolsthorpe.

For here at Woolsthorpe, Newton at the age of twenty-three made three of the greatest discoveries in science: the Differential Calculus, the Composition of Light, and the Laws of Gravitation. Writing towards the end of his life, Newton recalled his discovery of the laws of gravitation thus:

> In the same year (1666) I began to think of gravity extending to the orb of the moon . . . I deduced that the forces which keep the planets in their orbs must be reciprocally as the squares of their distances from the centers about which they revolve; and thereby compared the force requisite to keep the moon in her orb with the force of gravity at the surface of the earth, and found them answer pretty well. All this was in the two plague years 1665 and 1666, for in those days I was in the prime of my age for invention, and minded mathematics and philosophy more than at any time since.

Notice, first, his statement that "in those days . . . I minded mathematics and philosophy [meaning science] more than at any time since." Notice also the curious words "answer pretty well" to the agreement he had found with respect to the acceleration experienced by the moon in its orbit and as deduced—on the basis of his inverse-square law—from the acceleration experienced by bodies on the earth, that is, the falling apple. Newton does not appear to have felt any urgency to verify if his prediction "answers" more than "pretty well." Indeed, he does not seem to have experienced any special delight in having discovered so fundamental a law of nature. In actual fact, he dismissed the entire matter from his mind for a decade and more.

Newton returned to Cambridge early in 1667; and in 1669 he was appointed to the Lucasian Chair of Mathematics in succession to Barrow who had relinquished the Chair on Newton's behalf.

Soon after his return to Cambridge, Newton appears to have completed to his satisfaction his experimental investigations on the composition of light and constructed his first reflecting telescope to avoid the chromatic aberrations of the then extant refracting telescopes. But he did not publish any of these results of his investigations for several years.

The news of Newton having constructed a telescope on a new principle soon spread and Newton was urged to exhibit it at the Royal Society. It is known that Newton sent at least two telescopes to the Royal Society and that the second of them was exhibited in 1671.

Newton was elected to the Royal Society in January 1672. Stimulated perhaps by this recognition, Newton acceded to the request by Oldenburg, then the Secretary of the Royal Society, to communicate to the Society an account of his discoveries and in particular the principles underlying the construction of his telescope. In two successive letters, Newton replied to Oldenburg as follows:

> I shall endeavour to testify my gratitude by communicating what my poor and solitary endeavours can effect towards the promoting your philosophical designs. (January 6, 1672)

In the next letter he suggests communicating an account of his optical discoveries rather than a description of his telescope. He writes:

> An account of a philosophical discovery . . . which I doubt not but will prove much more grateful than the communication of that instrument, being in my judgement the oddest, if not the most considerable detection, which has hitherto been made in the operation of nature. (January 18, 1672)

I should like to draw your attention especially to the words, "the oddest, if not the most considerable detection." This is the first and the only time that Newton expresses a trace of enthusiasm with respect to any of his discoveries. But what followed the publication of Newton's account of his experiments on the composition of light was nothing short of a disaster. A vigorous controversy ensued, and Newton appears to have been irritated beyond endurance by the inability of his critics even to comprehend what it was he had experimentally demonstrated. This lack of comprehension is apparent, for example, from Huygens—even Huygens—arguing that there "would still remain the great difficulty of explaining by mechanical principles, in what consists the diversity of colours, even supposing that Newton's decomposition of white light into the colours of the spectrum is correct."

At first Newton tried to persuade by clarifying his method:

> For the best and safest method of philosophizing seems to be, first to enquire diligently into the properties of things, and of establishing those properties by experiments, and then to proceed more slowly to hypotheses for the explanation of them. For hypotheses should be subservient only in explaining the properties of things, but not assumed in determining them; unless so far as they may furnish experiments . . .

(Parenthetically, we may notice that Newton is, here, enunciating what he was to formulate later in his famous aphorism:

> *Hypotheses non fingo*—I frame no hypotheses.)

Newton's failure to persuade resulted in the aversion he now formed to scientific publication, discussion, and arguments. Thus, he wrote to Oldenburg:

I have long since determined to concern myself no further about the promotion of philosophy. (December 5, 1672)

I see I have made myself a slave to Philosophy, but if I get free of Mr. Linus' business I will resolutely bid adieu to it eternally, except what I do for my private satisfaction, or leave to come out after me. For I see, a man must either resolve to point out nothing new or to become a slave to defend it. (November 18, 1676)

This aversion to scientific publication, discussion, and argument was to find repeated expressions in later years. Here are two examples:

For I see not what there is desirable in public esteem, were I able to acquire and maintain it. It would perhaps increase my acquaintance, the thing which I chiefly study to decline.

I am grown of all men the most shy of setting pen to paper about anything that may lead into disputes. (September 12, 1682)

Soon after the publication of his optical discoveries, Newton receded into himself, and we do not know very much as to how he occupied himself during the following decade. But we do know that in 1679, Newton had proved for himself that under the influence of a central inverse-square attractive force an object will describe an elliptical orbit, with the center of attraction at one of its foci. But, again, he kept the result to himself.

At long last, in 1684, an incident, not of Newton's making, was to change the course of scientific history. In January of that year, at a meeting in London between Christopher Wren, Robert Hooke, and Edmund Halley, the question arose as to the nature of the orbit a planet would describe under the influence of an inverse-square attractive gravitational force. Since none of them knew how the question could be resolved, Halley went to Cambridge in August of that year to inquire if Newton had any suggestions to offer. To Halley's inquiry, Newton replied at once that the orbit would be an ellipse, and that he had established this result for himself some seven years earlier. Halley was overjoyed and wished to see Newton's proof. On Newton finding that he had mislaid the piece of paper on which he had written out the proof, he promised to rework it and send it to him shortly.

The reworking of this old problem seems to have aroused Newton's interest in the whole area. By October, he had worked out enough problems to serve as a basis for nine lectures which he gave during the Michaelmas term under the title *De Motu Corporum in gyrum*.

Halley, on receiving Newton's promised proof at about this time and hearing also of Newton's lectures, went to Cambridge once again, this time to persuade Newton to publish his lectures.

By now Newton's mathematical genius seems to have been fully aroused, and Newton appears to have been caught in its grip. Newton now entered upon a period of the most intense mathematical activity. Against his will and against his preferences, Newton seems to have been propelled inexorably forward, by the pressure of his own genius, till, at last, he had accomplished the greatest intellectual feat of his life, the greatest intellectual feat in all of science.

Let us pause for a moment to take full measure of the magnitude of this feat. By Newton's own account, he began writing the *Principia* towards the end of December 1684, and he sent the completed manuscript of all three Books of the *Principia* to the Royal Society in May 1686, that is, in seventeen months. He had solved two of the propositions in the first Book in 1679, and he had also proved eight of the propositions in the second Book in June and July 1685. There are ninety-eight propositions in the first Book; fifty-three in the second; and forty-two in the third. By far the larger proportion of them was, therefore, enunciated and proved during the seventeen consecutive months that Newton was at work on the three Books. It is this rapidity of execution, besides the monumental scale of the whole work, that makes this achievement incomparable. If the problems enunciated in the *Principia* were the results of a lifetime of thought and work, Newton's position in science would still be unique. But that all these problems should have been enunciated, solved, and arranged in logical sequence in seventeen months is beyond human comprehension. It can be accepted only because it is a fact: it just happens to be so!

It is only when we observe the scale of Newton's achievement that comparisons, which have sometimes been made with other men of science, appear altogether inappropriate both with respect to Newton and with respect to the others. In fact, only in juxtaposition with Shakespeare and Beethoven is the consideration of Newton appropriate.

Now, a few remarks concerning the style of the *Principia*. Quite unlike his early communications on his optical discoveries, the *Principia* is written in a style of glacial remoteness which makes no concessions to his readers. As Whewell aptly wrote:

> . . . As we read the *Principia,* we feel as when we are in an ancient armoury where the weapons are of gigantic size; and as we look at them, we marvel what manner of men they were who could use as weapons what we can scarcely lift as a burden . . .

It is, however, clear that the rigid and the lamellated style of the *Principia* is deliberate. For after the publication of the *Principia*, Newton is reported to have told Rev. Dr. Derham:

> To avoid being baited by little smatterers in mathematics, I designedly made the *Principia* abstruse; but yet so as to be understood by able mathematicians who, I imagine, by comprehending my demonstrations would concur with my theory.

Although Newton was only forty-two years of age when he finished writing the *Principia* and was, quite literally, at the height of his mathematical powers and was to remain in full possession of his faculties for another forty years, he never again seriously concerned himself with a scientific investigation. He turned to an utterly different way of living. And in time he became one of the principal sights of London for all visiting intellectuals: *the* Sir Isaac Newton of popular tradition.

No account of Newton's life, however brief, can omit some indication of the manner of man he was. The subject is a complex and a controversial one. But this much can fairly be said: Newton seems to have been remarkably insensitive: impervious to the arts, tactless, and with no real understanding of others.

Newton's most remarkable gift was probably his powers of concentration. As Keynes wrote:

> His peculiar gift was the power of holding continuously in his mind a purely mental problem until he had seen straight through it. I fancy his pre-eminence is due to his muscles of intuition being the strongest and most enduring with which a man has ever been gifted . . . I believe that Newton could hold a problem in his mind for hours and days and weeks until it surrendered to him its secret.

Besides, as De Morgan has said, he was:

> . . . So happy in his conjectures as to seem to know more than he could possibly have any means of proving.

But the central paradox of Newton's life is that he deliberately and systematically ignored his supreme mathematical genius and through most of his life neglected the one activity for which he was gifted beyond any man. This paradox can be resolved only if we realize that Newton simply did not consider science and mathematics as of any great importance; or, as Keynes has said:

> . . . It seems easier to understand . . . this strange spirit, who was tempted by the Devil to believe, at the time when within these walls

[of Trinity College] he was solving so much, that he could reach *all* the secrets of God and Nature by the pure power of mind—Copernicus and Faustus in one.

And finally, I cannot desist repeating Newton's oft-quoted evaluation of himself.

> I do not know what I may appear to the world, but to myself I seem to have been only like a boy playing on the sea-shore, and diverting myself in now and then finding a smoother pebble or a prettier shell than ordinary, whilst the great ocean of truth lay all undiscovered before me.

In view of Newton's insensitiveness to others, doubts have sometimes been raised about the sincerity of this statement. I do not believe that such doubts are warranted: only someone, like Newton, who can view knowledge from his height, can have the vision of an "ocean of undiscovered truth." As an ancient proverb of India says, "Only the wise can plumb the wells of wisdom."

IV

From the foregoing accounts of the creative patterns of Shakespeare, Beethoven, and Newton, though very brief and very inadequate, two facts emerge with startling clarity: the remarkable similarity in the creative patterns of Shakespeare and Beethoven, on the one hand, and their stark contrast with that of Newton, on the other. Are the similarity and the contrast accidental? Or, are they manifestations of a general phenomenon which in the case of these giants only happens to be very sharply etched?

Consider in juxtaposition the following statements that have been made concerning the creativity of mathematicians and of poets.

G. H. Hardy, an outstanding English mathematician of this century, in his essay *A Mathematician's Apology*—an essay which has been described by C. P. Snow as "the most beautiful statement of the creative mind ever written or ever likely to be written"—writes:

> No mathematician should ever allow himself to forget that mathematics, more than any other art or science, is a young man's game . . . Galois died at twenty-one, Abel at twenty-seven, Ramanujan at thirty-three, Riemann at forty. There have been men who have done great work a good deal later; . . . [but] I do not know an instance of a major mathematical advance initiated by a man past fifty. . . . A mathematician may still be competent enough at sixty, but it is useless to expect him to have original ideas.

And with respect to Ramanujan's early death, Hardy has further written:

> The real tragedy about Ramanujan was not his early death. It is, of course, a disaster that any great man should die young; but a mathematician is comparatively old at thirty, and his death may be less of a catastrophe than it seems . . .

Place beside these statements of Hardy the following one of A. L. Rowse on the death of Christopher Marlowe at the age of twenty-nine:

> What would he not have achieved if he had lived!—his was the greatest of all losses to English Literature.

Or, of Desmond King-Hele's on the death of Shelley at the age of thirty:

> The rule that a poet is at his best after the age of 30 might have applied as well to him as to Shakespeare, Milton, Wordsworth, Byron, Tennyson, and indeed almost every major English poet who lived to be over 30.

In a more negative vein, there is the statement attributed to Thomas Huxley that a man of science past sixty does more harm than good.

I do not doubt that these statements will be challenged or, at least, subjected to qualifications. But consider this.

In 1817, at the age of forty-seven, when the long period of meditation, during which Beethoven composed very little, was coming to an end, he said to Cipriani Potter with transparent sincerity, "*Now,* I know how to compose." I do not believe that there has been any scientist, past forty, who could have said, "*Now,* I know how to do research." And this to my mind is the center and the core of the difference: the apparent inability of a scientist to continually grow and mature.

V

If one should wish to establish with some degree of certainty that a contrast does exist in the patterns of creativity among the practitioners in the arts and the practitioners in the sciences, then one should undertake a survey of an extent and a depth which is far beyond my resources. At the same time it does not seem entirely proper that I leave the matter without some further examples. I shall consider four examples taken from science.

My first example is James Clerk Maxwell who is generally considered the greatest physicist of the nineteenth century. Maxwell's principal contributions to physics are his founding of the kinetic theory of gases and the dynamical theory of the electromagnetic field. The new physical concepts which Maxwell introduced in formulating his equations of the electromagnetic field—Maxwell's equations which every student of physics knows—have been described by Einstein as "the most fruitful and profound that physics has experienced since the time of Newton."

The four great memoirs which encompass Maxwell's contributions to the two areas were published during the five years 1860–65 when he was between the ages of thirty and thirty-five and was a professor at King's College, London. At the end of this period of intense activity, Maxwell resigned his professorship in London and retired to his country home in Glenlair in Scotland. (Maxwell's biographers never really "explain" why Maxwell felt it necessary to take these actions.) In Glenlair, for the following six years, Maxwell seems to have lived in quietness, occupied, principally, with the planning of his two-volume *Treatise on Electricity and Magnetism* (which was eventually completed and published in 1873). In 1871, Maxwell was persuaded to leave his retirement in Glenlair and return to academic life in Cambridge as the first Cavendish Professor of Experimental Physics. He died in 1878 at the age of forty-eight. Maxwell's eight years in Cambridge were devoted mostly to editing the scientific papers of Henry Cavendish, organizing and establishing the Cavendish Laboratory, and other diverse university matters. While Maxwell's early death was a tragedy, it must be admitted that his work did not rise again to the heights it had in his early thirties.

My second example is George Gabriel Stokes. Stokes was elected to the Lucasian Chair of Mathematics (in Cambridge) in 1849 when he was just past thirty. He held this Chair until his death in 1903—a Chair that was once held by Newton. Stokes is one of the great figures of nineteenth-century physics and mathematics. His name continues to be associated with several current notions and concepts. Thus, we have the Navier-Stokes equations governing viscous flow in hydrodynamics; the Stokes law giving the asymptotic rate of fall of small spherical bodies in a viscous medium—a law which provides the basis for Millikan's "oil-drop experiment" for determining the charge on the electron; the Stokes parameters for characterizing polarized radiation which are relevant to most current measurements in radio-astronomy; the Stokes law of fluorescence, that the wavelength of the fluorescing light must exceed that of the exciting light; and the Stokes theorem which, in addition to being a very fundamental theorem, provides a key element for modern developments in the calculus of differential forms.

Now Stokes's scientific papers are collected in five medium-sized volumes. The first three volumes contain all the important concepts and notions that I have just enumerated and cover the ten-year period 1842–52; the remaining two volumes suffice to cover his entire scientific work of the following fifty years.

G. Evelyn Hutchinson (the distinguished zoologist at Yale University), whose father was a close associate of Stokes during his last years, makes the remarkable statement: "Stokes, however, quite possibly, emulated his great predecessor [in the Lucasian Chair] consciously. . . . What Newton did, Stokes deemed appropriate for him to do also."

My third example is Einstein. The year 1905 was the *annus mirabilis* both for Einstein and for physics. It was in that year that Einstein, at the age of twenty-six, published three papers, each epoch-making in its own way: the first laid the foundations for his special theory of relativity with remarkable clarity, conciseness, and coherence; the second provided a rational molecular basis (independently of Smoluchowski) for accounting for Brownian motion; and the third carried Planck's hypothesis of the quantum to its logical limit to formulate the concept of the light quantum. In the decade that followed, Einstein was constantly preoccupied with the resolution of the basic inconsistency between Newton's law of gravitation, with its postulate of instantaneous action at a distance, and his own special theory of relativity, with its postulate that no signal can be propagated with a velocity exceeding that of light. After many detours and false starts, Einstein finally arrived triumphantly at his general theory of relativity in 1915. As Hermann Weyl later expressed, Einstein's general theory of relativity is "one of the great examples of the power of speculative thought."

In the years following the founding of his general theory of relativity, Einstein made a number of important contributions to the further ramifications of his own general theory as well as to certain aspects of statistical physics. But already by 1925, Einstein was letting the newer developments in the quantum theory, initiated by Heisenberg, pass him by. Thus, Heisenberg records that at the Solvay Congress in 1927, Paul Ehrenfest, Einstein's friend, said to him, "Einstein, I am ashamed of you: you are arguing against the new quantum theory just as your opponents argue about relativity theory." Heisenberg adds sadly that this friendly admonition went unheeded. As Einstein's great admirer Cornelius Lanczos observes

From 1925 on his interest in the current affairs of physics begins to slacken. He voluntarily abdicated his leadership as the foremost physicist of his time, and receded more and more into voluntary exile from his laboratory, a state into which only a few of his colleagues were willing to follow. During the last thirty years of his life he became more and more a recluse who lost touch with the contemporary developments of physics.

I should like to conclude with an example which in some ways appears counter to Hardy's general rule: the case of Lord Rayleigh, perhaps the greatest pillar of classical mathematical physics. Rayleigh's productivity was remarkably steady and uniform all through his fifty years of scientific publication. His scientific work is encompassed in a two-volume treatise on *The Theory of Sound* and the six large volumes of his *Scientific Papers*.

In a memorial address, delivered in Westminster Abbey in December 1921, J. J. Thomson evaluated Rayleigh's scientific contributions in the following terms:

> Among the 446 papers which fill these volumes [the six volumes of his *Scientific Papers*], there is not one that is trivial, there is not one which does not advance the subject with which it deals, there is not one which does not clear away difficulties; and among that great number there are scarcely any which time has shown to require correction . . . Lord Rayleigh took physics for his province and extended the boundary of every department of physics. The impression made by reading his papers is not only due to the beauty of the new results attained, but to the clearness and insight displayed, which gives one a new grasp of the subject . . .

This is a remarkable testimony; and anyone who has had occasion to use Rayleigh's *Scientific Papers* will testify to its accuracy.

But why was Rayleigh so different from Maxwell and Einstein? Perhaps the clue is to be found in what Thomson said in the same memorial address:

> There are some great men of science whose charm consists in having said the first word on a subject, in having introduced some new idea which has proved fruitful; there are others whose charm consists perhaps in having said the last word on the subject, and who have reduced the subject to logical consistency and clearness. I think by temperament Lord Rayleigh belonged to the second group.

And perhaps there is a clue also in Rayleigh's response to his son (also a distinguished physicist) when he asked him to comment on Huxley's remark I quoted earlier, "that a man of science past sixty does more harm than good." Rayleigh was sixty-seven at that time, and his response was

That may be, if he undertakes to criticize the work of younger men, but I do not see why it need be so if he sticks to the things he is conversant with.

Perhaps there is a moral here for all of us!

VI

I now pass on to some cognate matters.

First, may I say that I am frankly puzzled by the difference that appears to exist in the patterns of creativity among the practitioners in the arts and the practitioners in the sciences: for, in the arts as in the sciences, the quest is after the same elusive quality: beauty. But what is beauty?

In a deeply moving essay on "The Meaning of Beauty in the Exact Sciences," Heisenberg gives a definition of beauty which I find most apposite. The definition, which Heisenberg says goes back to antiquity, is that "beauty is the proper conformity of the parts to one another and to the whole." On reflection, it does appear that this definition touches the essence of what we may describe as "beautiful": it applies equally to *King Lear,* the *Missa Solemnis,* and the *Principia.*

There is ample evidence that in science, beauty is often the source of delight. One can find many expressions of such delight scattered through the scientific literature. Let me quote a few examples.

Kepler:

> Mathematics is the archetype of the beautiful.

David Hilbert (in his memorial address for Hermann Minkowski):

> Our Science, which we loved above everything, had brought us together. It appeared to us as a flowering garden. In this garden there were well-worn paths where one might look around at leisure and enjoy oneself without effort, especially at the side of a congenial companion. But we also liked to seek out hidden trails and discovered many an unexpected view which was pleasing to our eyes; and when the one pointed it out to the other, and we admired it together, our joy was complete.

Hermann Weyl (as quoted by Freeman Dyson):

> My work always tried to unite the true with the beautiful; but when I had to choose one or the other, I usually chose the beautiful.

Heisenberg (in a discussion with Einstein):

If nature leads us to mathematical forms of great simplicity and beauty—by forms I am referring to coherent systems of hypothesis, axioms, etc.—to forms that no one has previously encountered, we cannot help thinking that they are "true," that they reveal a genuine feature of nature . . . You must have felt this too: the almost frightening simplicity and wholeness of the relationships which nature suddenly spreads out before us and for which none of us was in the least prepared.

All these quotations express thoughts that may appear vague or too general. Let me try to be concrete and specific.

The discovery by Pythagoras, that vibrating strings, under equal tension, sound together harmoniously if their lengths are in simple numerical ratios, established for the first time a profound connection between the intelligible and the beautiful. I think we may agree with Heisenberg that this is "one of the truly momentous discoveries in the history of mankind."

Kepler was certainly under the influence of the Pythagorean concept of beauty when he compared the revolution of the planets about the sun with a vibrating string and spoke of the harmonious concord of the different planetary orbits as the music of the spheres. It is known that Kepler was profoundly grateful that it had been reserved for him to discover, through his laws of planetary motion, a connection of the highest beauty.

A more recent example of the reaction of a great scientist, to this aspect of beauty at the moment of revelation of a great truth, is provided by Heisenberg's description of the state of his feelings when he found the key that opened the door to all the subsequent developments in the quantum theory.

Towards the end of May 1925, Heisenberg, ill with hay fever, went to Heligoland to be away from flowers and fields. There by the sea, he made rapid progress in resolving the difficulties in the quantum theory as it was at that time. He writes:

Within a few days more, it had become clear to me what precisely had to take the place of the Bohr-Sommerfeld quantum conditions in an atomic physics working with none but observable magnitudes. It also became obvious that with this additional assumption, I had introduced a crucial restriction into the theory. Then I noticed that there was no guarantee that . . . the principle of the conservation of energy would apply . . . Hence I concentrated on demonstrating that the conservation law held; and one evening I reached the point where I was ready to determine the individual terms in the energy table [Energy Matrix] . . . When the first terms seemed to accord with the energy principle, I became rather excited, and I began to make countless arithmetical errors.

As a result, it was almost three o'clock in the morning before the final result of my computations lay before me. The energy principle had held for all the terms, and I could no longer doubt the mathematical consistency and coherence of the kind of quantum mechanics to which my calculations pointed. At first, I was deeply alarmed. I had the feeling that, through the surface of atomic phenomena, I was looking at a strangely beautiful interior, and felt almost giddy at the thought that I now had to probe this wealth of mathematical structure nature had so generously spread out before me. I was far too excited to sleep, and so, as a new day dawned, I made for the southern tip of the island, where I had been longing to climb a rock jutting out into the sea. I now did so without too much trouble, and waited for the sun to rise.

May I allow myself at this point a personal reflection? In my entire scientific life, extending over forty-five years, the most shattering experience has been the realization that an exact solution of Einstein's equations of general relativity, discovered by the New Zealand mathematician, Roy Kerr, provides the *absolutely exact representation* of untold numbers of massive black holes that populate the universe. This "shuddering before the beautiful," this incredible fact that a discovery motivated by a search after the beautiful in mathematics should find its exact replica in Nature, persuades me to say that beauty is that to which the human mind responds at its deepest and most profound. Indeed, everything I have tried to say in this connection has been stated more succinctly in the Latin mottos:

Simplex sigillum veri—The simple is the seal of the true.

and

Pulchritudo splendor veritatis—Beauty is the splendour of truth.

VII

But I must return to my question: why is there a difference in the patterns of creativity among the practitioners in the arts and the practitioners in the sciences? I shall not attempt to answer this question directly; but I shall make an assortment of remarks which may bear on the answer.

First, I should like to consider how scientists and poets view one another. When one thinks of the attitude of the poets to science, one almost always thinks of Wordsworth and Keats and their oft-quoted lines:

A fingering slave,
One that would peep and botanize
Upon his mother's grave?

A reasoning self-sufficing thing,
An intellectual All-in-all!

Sweet is the lore which Nature brings;
    Our meddling intellect
Misshapes the beauteous forms of things:
    We murder to dissect.
                                    (Wordsworth)

        Do not all charms fly
At the mere touch of cold philosophy?
There was an awful rainbow once in heaven:
We know her woof, her texture; she is given
In the dull catalogue of common things.
Philosophy will clip an Angel's wings.
                                    (Keats)

These lines, perhaps, find an echo in a statement of Lowes Dickinson, "When Science arrives, it expels Literature."

It is to be expected that one should find scientists countering these views. Thus, Peter Medawar counters Lowes Dickinson by

> The case I shall find evidence for is that when literature arrives, it expels science . . . The way things are at present, it is simply no good pretending that science and literature represent complementary and mutually sustaining endeavours to reach a common goal. On the contrary, where they might be expected to cooperate, they compete.

It would not seem to me that one can go very far in these matters by pointing accusing fingers at one another. So, let me only say that the attitudes of Wordsworth and Keats are by no means typical. A scientist should rather consider the attitude of Shelley. Shelley is a scientist's poet. It is not an accident that the most discriminating literary criticism of Shelley's thought and work is by a distinguished scientist, Desmond King-Hele. As King-Hele has pointed out, "Shelley's attitude to science emphasizes the surprising modern climate of thought in which he chose to live," and Shelley "describes the mechanisms of Nature with a precision and a wealth of detail unparalleled in English poetry." And here is A. N. Whitehead's testimony:

> Shelley's attitude to Science was at the opposite pole to that of Wordsworth. He loved it, and is never tired of expressing in poetry the

thoughts which it suggests. It symbolizes to him joy, and peace, and illumination . . .

I should like to read two examples from Shelley's poetry which support what has been said about him. The first example is from his *Cloud* which "fuses together a creative myth, a scientific monograph, and a gay picaresque tale of cloud adventure":

> I am the daughter of Earth and Water,
>   And the nursling of the Sky;
> I pass through the pores of the ocean and shores;
>   I change, but I cannot die.
> For after the rain when with never a stain
>   The pavilion of Heaven is bare,
> And the winds and sunbeams with their convex gleams
>   Build up the blue dome of air,
> I silently laugh at my own cenotaph,
>   And out of the caverns of rain,
> Like a child from the womb, like a ghost from the tomb,
>   I arise and unbuild it again.

The second example is from *Prometheus Unbound,* which has been described by Herbert Read as "the greatest expression ever given to humanity's desire for intellectual light and spiritual liberty":

> The lightning is his slave; heaven's utmost deep
> Gives up her stars, and like a flock of sheep
> They pass before his eye, are numbered, and roll on!
>   The tempest is his steed, he strides the air;
>   And the abyss shouts from her depth laid bare,
> Heaven, hast thou secrets? Man unveils me; I have none.

Let me turn to a slightly different aspect of the matter. What are we to make of the following confession of Charles Darwin:

> Up to the age of thirty, or beyond it, poetry of many kinds, such as the works of Milton, Gray, Byron, Wordsworth, Coleridge, and Shelley, gave me great pleasure; and even as a school boy I took intense delight in Shakespeare, especially historical plays . . . I have also said that formerly pictures gave me considerable, and music very great delight. But now for many years I cannot endure to read a line of poetry; I have tried lately to read Shakespeare, and found it so intolerably dull that it nauseated me. I have almost lost my taste for pictures or music . . . My mind seems to have become a kind of machine for grinding general laws out of large collections of facts, but why this should have caused the atrophy of that part of the brain alone on which the higher tastes depend, I cannot conceive.

Or, consider this: Faraday discovered the laws of electromagnetic in-
duction, and his discoveries led him to formulate concepts such as
"lines of force" and "fields of force" which were foreign to the then-
prevailing modes of thought. They were in fact looked askance by
many of his contemporaries. But of Faraday's ideas, Maxwell wrote
with prophetic discernment:

> The way in which Faraday made use of his idea of lines of force in
> coordinating the phenomenon of magneto-electric induction shows him
> to have been in reality a mathematician of a very high order—one from
> whom the mathematicians of the future may derive valuable and fertile
> methods. We are probably ignorant even of the name of the science
> which will be developed out of the materials we are now collecting,
> when the great philosopher next after Faraday makes his appearance.

And yet when Gladstone, then the Chancellor of the Exchequer, interrupted Faraday in his description of his work on electricity by the
impatient inquiry, "But after all, what use is it?" Faraday's response
was, "Why, Sir, there is every probability that you will soon be able
to tax it." And Faraday's response has always been quoted most
approvingly.

It seems to me that to Darwin's confession and to Faraday's response, what Shelley has said about the cultivation of the sciences in
his *A Defence of Poetry* is apposite:

> The cultivation of those sciences which have enlarged the limits of the
> empire of man over the external world, has, for want of the poetical
> faculty, proportionally circumscribed those of the internal world; and
> man, having enslaved the elements, remains himself a slave.

Lest you think that Shelley is not sensitive to the role of technology in
modern society, let me quote what he has said in that connection:

> Undoubtedly the promoters of utility, in this limited sense, have their
> appointed office in society. They follow the footstep of poets, and copy
> the sketches of their creations into the book of common life. They make
> space, and give time.

Shelley's *A Defence of Poetry* from which I have just quoted is one
of the most moving documents in all of English literature. W. B. Yeats
has called it "the profoundest essay on the foundation of poetry in the
English language." The essay should be read in its entirety; but allow
me to read a selection:

> Poetry is the record of the best and happiest moments of the happiest
> and best minds.

Poetry thus makes immortal all that is best and most beautiful in the world; it arrests the vanishing apparitions which haunt the interlunations of life . . .

Poetry is indeed something divine. It is at once the centre and circumference of knowledge; it is that which comprehends all science, and that to which all science must be referred. It is at the same time the root and blossom of all other systems of thought.

Poets are the hierophants of an unapprehended inspiration; the mirrors of the gigantic shadows which futurity casts upon the present; the words which express what they understand not; the trumpets which sing to battle, and feel not what they inspire; the influence which is moved not, but moves. Poets are the unacknowledged legislators of the world.

On reading Shelley's *A Defence of Poetry,* the question insistently occurs why there is no similar *A Defence of Science* written by a scientist of equal endowment. Perhaps in raising this question I have, in part, suggested an answer to the one I have repeatedly asked during the lecture.

I began this lecture by asking your forbearance for addressing myself to matters which are largely outside the circumference of my comprehension. Allow me then to conclude by quoting from Shakespeare's epilogue to the second part of his *Henry IV:*

First, my fear; then my curtsy; last my speech. My fear, is your displeasure, my curtsy, my duty, and my speech, to beg your pardon.

4

Beauty and the Quest for Beauty in Science

The topic to which I have been asked to address myself is a difficult one, if one is to avoid the trivial and the banal. Besides, my knowledge and my experience, such as they are, compel me to limit myself, entirely, to the theoretical aspects of the physical sciences—limitations, most serious. I must, therefore, begin by asking for your patience and your forbearance.

All of us are sensitive to Nature's beauty. It is not unreasonable that some aspects of this beauty are shared by the natural sciences. But one may ask the question as to the extent to which the quest for beauty is an aim in the pursuit of science. On this question, Poincaré is unequivocal. In one of his essays he has written:

> The Scientist does not study nature because it is useful to do so. He studies it because he takes pleasure in it; and he takes pleasure in it because it is beautiful. If nature were not beautiful, it would not be worth knowing and life would not be worth living. . . . I mean the intimate beauty which comes from the harmonious order of its parts and which a pure intelligence can grasp.

And Poincaré goes on to say,

This lecture was given at the International Symposium in honor of Robert R. Wilson on 27 April 1979 at the Fermi National Accelerator Laboratory, Batavia, Illinois. It was later published in *Aesthetics and Science: Proceedings of the International Symposium in Honor of Robert R. Wilson, April 27, 1979* by the Fermi National Accelerator Laboratory, and also in *Physics Today* 32 (1979): 25. It is reprinted here with the permission of the Fermi National Accelerator Laboratory.

It is because simplicity and vastness are both beautiful that we seek by preference simple facts and vast facts; that we take delight, now in following the giant courses of the stars, now in scrutinizing with a microscope that prodigious smallness which is also a vastness, and, now in seeking in geological ages the traces of the past that attracts us because of its remoteness.

Commenting on these observations of Poincaré, J. W. N. Sullivan, the author of perceptive biographies of both Newton and Beethoven, wrote (in the *Athenaeum* for May 1919):

Since the primary object of the scientific theory is to express the harmonies which are found to exist in nature, we see at once that these theories must have an aesthetic value. The measure of the success of a scientific theory is, in fact, a measure of its aesthetic value, since it is a measure of the extent to which it has introduced harmony in what was before chaos.

It is in its aesthetic value that the justification of the scientific theory is to be found, and with it the justification of the scientific method. Since facts without laws would be of no interest, and laws without theories would have, at most, only a practical utility, we see that the motives which guide the scientific man are, from the beginning, manifestations of the aesthetic impulse. . . . The measure in which science falls short of art is the measure in which it is incomplete as science.

In a perceptive essay on "Art and Science," the distinguished art critic, Roger Fry (who may be known to some of you through Virginia Woolf's biography of him), begins by quoting Sullivan and continues:

Sullivan boldly says: "It is in its aesthetic value that the justification of the scientific theory is to be found, and with it the justification of the scientific method." I should like to pose to S. [Sullivan] at this point the question whether a theory that disregarded facts would have equal value for science with one which agreed with facts. I suppose he would say No; and yet so far as I can see there would be no purely aesthetic reason why it should not.

I shall return to this question which Roger Fry raises and suggest an answer different from what Fry presumes that Sullivan would have given. But I shall pass on now to Fry's observations comparing the impulses of an artist and of a scientist.

From the merest rudiments of pure sensation up to the highest efforts of design, each point in the process of art is inevitably accompanied by pleasure: it cannot proceed without it. . . . It is also true that the recognition of inevitability in thought is normally accompanied by pleasurable emotion; and that the desire for this mental pleasure is the motive force which impels to the making of scientific theory. In science the inevitability of the relations remains equally definite and demonstrable, whether the emotion accompanies it or not, whereas, in art, an aesthetic harmony simply does not exist without the emotional state. The harmony in art is not true unless it is felt with emotion. . . . In art the recognition of relations is immediate and sensational—perhaps we ought to consider it curiously akin to those cases of mathematical geniuses who have immediate intuition of mathematical relations which it is beyond their powers to prove.

Let me pass on from these generalities to particular examples of what scientists have responded to as beautiful.

My first example is related to Fry's observation with respect to what mathematical geniuses perceive as true with no apparent cause. The Indian mathematician Srinivasa Ramanujan (whose dramatic emergence into mathematical fame in 1915 may be known to some of you) left a large number of notebooks (one of which was discovered only a few years ago). In these notebooks Ramanujan has recorded several hundred formulae and identities. Many of these have been proved only recently by methods which Ramanujan could not have known. G. N. Watson, who spent several years of his life proving many of Ramanujan's identities, has written:

The study of Ramanujan's work and the problem to which it gives rise, inevitably recalls to mind Lamé's remark that, when reading Hermite's papers on modular functions, "*on a la chair de poule.*" I would express my own attitude with more prolixity by saying that such a formula as,

$$\int_0^\infty e^{-3\pi x^2} \frac{\sinh\pi x}{\sinh 3\pi x}\, dx = \frac{1}{e^{2\pi/3}\sqrt{3}} \sum_{n=0}^\infty e^{-2n(n+1)\pi}(1 + e^{-\pi})^{-2}$$
$$\times\, (1 + e^{-3\pi})^{-2} \ldots (1 + e^{-(2n+1)\pi})^{-2},$$

gives me a thrill which is indistinguishable from the thrill which I feel when I enter the Sagrestia Nuova of Capelle Medicee and see before me the austere beauty of "Day," "Night," "Evening," and "Dawn" which Michelangelo has set over the tombs of Giuliano de' Medici and Lorenzo de' Medici.

An example of a very different kind is provided by Boltzmann's reaction to one of Maxwell's papers on the dynamical theory of gases in which Maxwell shows how one can solve exactly for the transport coefficients in a gas in which the intermolecular force varies as the inverse fifth power of the intermolecular distance. Here is Boltzmann:

The Medici tombs, designed by Michelangelo, with figures representing Night, Day, Evening, and Dawn.

Even as a musician can recognize his Mozart, Beethoven, or Schubert after hearing the first few bars, so can a mathematician recognize his Cauchy, Gauss, Jacobi, Helmholtz, or Kirchhoff after the first few pages. The French writers reveal themselves by their extreme formal elegance, while the English, especially Maxwell, by their dramatic sense. Who, for example, is not familiar with Maxwell's memoirs on his dynamical theory of gases? . . . The variations of the velocities are, at first, developed majestically; then from one side enter the equations of state; and from the other side, the equations of motion in a central field. Ever higher soars the chaos of formulae. Suddenly, we hear, as from kettle drums, the four beats "put $n = 5$." The evil spirit V (the relative velocity of the two molecules) vanishes; and, even as in music, a hitherto dominating figure in the bass is suddenly silenced, that which had seemed insuperable has been overcome as if by a stroke of magic. . . . This is not the time to ask why this or that substitution. If you are not swept along with the development, lay aside the paper. Maxwell does not write programme music with explanatory notes. . . . One result after another follows in quick succession till at last, as the unexpected climax, we arrive at the conditions for thermal equilibrium together with the expressions for the transport coefficients. The curtain then falls!

I have started with these two simple examples to emphasize that one does not have to go to the largest canvasses to find beauty in science. But the largest canvasses do provide the best examples. I shall consider two of them.

Einstein's discovery of the general theory of relativity has been described by Hermann Weyl as a supreme example of the power of speculative thought, while Landau and Lifschitz consider the theory as probably the most beautiful of all existing physical theories. And Einstein himself wrote at the end of his first paper announcing his field equations: "Scarcely anyone who fully comprehends this theory can escape from its magic." I shall return later to consider wherein the source of this magic lies. Meantime, I want to contrast, in parallel with Einstein's expressed reaction to his theory, the feelings of Heisenberg at the moment of his discovery of quantum mechanics. We are fortunate in having Heisenberg's own account. He writes:

. . . it had become clear to me what precisely had to take the place of the Bohr-Sommerfeld quantum conditions in an atomic physics working with none but observable magnitudes. It also became obvious that with this additional assumption, I had introduced a crucial restriction into the theory. Then I noticed that there was no guarantee that . . . the principle of the conservation of energy would apply . . . Hence I concentrated on demonstrating that the conservation law held; and one evening I reached the point where I was ready to determine the individual terms in the energy table [Energy Matrix] . . . When the first terms seemed to accord with the energy principle, I became rather excited, and I began to make countless arithmetical errors. As a result, it was almost three o'clock in the morning before the final result of my computations lay before me. The energy principle had held for all the terms, and I could no longer doubt the mathematical consistency and coherence of the kind of quantum mechanics to which my calculations pointed. At first, I was deeply alarmed. I had the feeling that, through the surface of atomic phenomena, I was looking at a strangely beautiful interior, and felt almost giddy at the thought that I now had to probe this wealth of mathematical structure nature had so generously spread out before me.

In the context of these statements by Einstein and by Heisenberg on their discoveries, it is of interest to recall the following conversation between Heisenberg and Einstein which Heisenberg has recorded. Here is an extract:

If nature leads us to mathematical forms of great simplicity and beauty—by forms I am referring to coherent systems of hypotheses, axioms, etc.—to forms that no one has previously encountered, we cannot help thinking that they are "true," that they reveal a genuine feature of nature . . . You must have felt this too: the almost frightening simplicity and wholeness of the relationships which nature suddenly spreads out before us and for which none of us was in the least prepared.

These remarks of Heisenberg find an echo in the following lines of Keats:

Beauty is truth,
    truth beauty—that is all
Ye know on earth,
    and all ye need to know.

At this point, I should like to return to Roger Fry's question I quoted earlier, namely, what one should make of a theory which is aesthetically satisfying but which one believes is not true.

Freeman Dyson has quoted Weyl as having told him: "My work always tried to unite the true with the beautiful; but when I had to choose one or the other, I usually chose the beautiful." I inquired of Dyson whether Weyl had given an example of his having sacrificed truth for beauty. I learned that the example which Weyl gave was his gauge theory of gravitation, which he had worked out in his *Raum-*

Zeit-Materie. Apparently, Weyl became convinced that this theory was not true as a theory of gravitation; but still it was so beautiful that he did not wish to abandon it and so he kept it alive for the sake of its beauty. But much later, it did turn out that Weyl's instinct was right after all, when the formalism of gauge invariance was incorporated into quantum electrodynamics.

Another example which Weyl did not mention, but to which Dyson drew attention, is Weyl's two-component relativistic wave equation of the neutrino. Weyl discovered this equation and the physicists ignored it for some thirty years because it violated parity invariance. And again, it turned out that Weyl's instincts were right.

We have evidence, then, that a theory developed by a scientist, with an exceptionally well-developed aesthetic sensibility, can turn out to be true even if, at the time of its formulation, it appeared not to be so. As Keats wrote a long time ago, "what the imagination seizes as beauty must be truth—whether it existed before or not."

It is, indeed, an incredible fact that what the human mind, at its deepest and most profound, perceives as beautiful finds its realization in external nature.

What is intelligible is also beautiful.

We may well ask: how does it happen that beauty in the exact sciences becomes recognizable even before it is understood in detail and before it can be rationally demonstrated? In what does this power of illumination consist?

These questions have puzzled many thinkers from the earliest times. Thus, Heisenberg has drawn attention, precisely in this connection, to the following thought expressed by Plato in the *Phaedrus:*

> The soul is awestricken and shudders at the sight of the beautiful, for it feels that something is evoked in it that was not imparted to it from without by the senses, but has always been already laid down there in the deeply unconscious region.

The same thought is expressed in the following aphorism of David Hume: "Beauty in things exists in the mind which contemplates them."

Kepler was so struck by the harmony of nature as revealed to him by his discovery of the laws of planetary motion that in his *Harmony of the World,* he wrote:

> Now, it might be asked how this faculty of the soul, which does not engage in conceptual thinking and can therefore have no prior knowledge of harmonic relations, should be capable of recognizing what is given in the outward world. . . . To this, I answer that all pure Ideas, or arche-

typal patterns of harmony, such as we are speaking of, are inherently present in those who are capable of apprehending them. But they are not first received into the mind by a conceptual process, being the product, rather, of a sort of instinctive intuition and innate to those individuals.

More recently, Pauli, elaborating on these ideas of Kepler, has written:

> The bridge, leading from the initially unordered data of experience to the Ideas, consists in certain primeval images pre-existing in the soul—the archetypes of Kepler. These primeval images should not be located in consciousness or related to specific rationally formulizable ideas. It is a question, rather, of forms belonging to the unconscious region of the human soul, images of powerful emotional content, which are not thought, but beheld, as it were, pictorially. The delight one feels, on becoming aware of a new piece of knowledge, arises from the way such pre-existing images fall into congruence with the behavior of the external objects.

Pauli concludes,

> One should never declare that theses laid down by rational formulation are the only possible presuppositions of human reason.

This congruence between preexisting images and external reality, to which Pauli refers, once intensely experienced appears to have the consequence that it develops overconfidence in judgment and values in the person who has had such an experience. For otherwise, how can one understand statements, such as these, made by some of the great scientists:

"It is thermodynamics gone mad," by Lord Kelvin, one of the founders of thermodynamics, commenting on Boltzmann's derivation of Wien's and Stefan's law.

"You look at it from the point of view of the star; I look at it from the point of view of Nature," by Eddington in a controversial discussion with me.

"I disagree with most physicists at the present time just at this point," by Dirac in the context of his views on the extant methods of renormalization in quantum electrodynamics.

"It really looked as if, for the first time, we had a framework wide enough to include the entire spectrum of elementary particles and their interactions, fulfilling my dream of 1933," by Heisenberg in 1957 in the context of his ill-fated collaboration with Pauli on a unified field theory.

"God does not throw dice," by Einstein; or, even more provokingly, "When judging a physical theory, I ask myself whether I would have made the Universe in that way had I been God," also by Einstein.

In the context of these last statements by Einstein, it may be well to remember Bohr's remonstrance "Nor is it our business to prescribe to God how he should run the world!"

Perhaps it is in terms of this overconfidence that one must try to understand the comparative sterility of once great minds. For as Claude Bernard has said, "Those who have an excessive faith in their ideas are not fitted to make discoveries." I am clearly treading on dangerous ground. But it does provide me the opportunity to draw attention to a fact which has been a source of considerable puzzlement to me: it concerns the very different ways—at least, so they seem to me—in which great writers, poets, and musicians, on the one hand, and great scientists, on the other, appear to grow and to mature.

It is not uncommon that in considering the works of a great writer or a great composer one distinguishes an early, a middle, and a late period. And it is almost always the case that the progression from the early, to the middle, and to the late periods is one of growing depth and excellence. In some cases, as in the cases of Shakespeare and Beethoven, the latest works are the greatest. This fact is forcibly described by J. Dover Wilson in his delineation of the growth of Shakespeare's art in his great tragedies.

> From 1601 to 1608 he is absorbed in tragedy; and the path he treads during these eight years may be likened to a mountain track which, rising gently from the plain, grows ever narrower, until at the climax of the ascent it dwindles to the thinnest razor-edge, a glacial arete, with the abyss on either hand, and then once again grows secure for foothold as it broadens out and gradually descends into the valley beyond.
>
> Eight plays compose this tragic course. The first, *Julius Caesar,* written a little before the tragic period proper, is a tragedy of weakness not of evil. In *Hamlet* the forces of evil are active and sinister, though still the prevailing note is weakness of character. *Othello* gives Shakespeare's earliest creation of a character wholly evil, and at the same time Iago's victim is blameless—human weakness is no longer allowed to share the responsibility with heaven. *King Lear* carries us right to the edge of the abyss, for here horror is piled upon horror and pity on pity, to make

the greatest monument of human misery and despair in the literature of the world. . . . Shakespeare came very near to madness in *Lear*.

Yet he pushed forward: *Macbeth, Antony and Cleopatra* (one of the very greatest of Shakespeare's plays), and *Coriolanus* followed in succession. And Dover Wilson asks: "How did Shakespeare save his soul alive in this, one of the most perilous and arduous adventures ever undertaken by the spirit of man?" Shakespeare survived; and he survived only to follow his great tragedies by those wonderful plays, *Winter's Tale* and *The Tempest*.

I am afraid that I have, perhaps, digressed a little too long in detailing to you the growth of Shakespeare's art. But I did want to emphasize to you the magnitude of that growth. And I am sure that one can say very similar things about Beethoven's late compositions which include the *Hammerklavier Sonata,* the *Missa Solemnis,* and above all, his last quartets.

While Shakespeare and Beethoven are probably unique in treading the razor-edge at the very end of their lives and surviving, there are others who illustrate, at a somewhat more modest level, the same consistent ascent to higher peaks of accomplishment. But I am not aware of a single instance of a scientist of whom the same can be said. His early successes are often his last successes. (I am here excluding the cases of those who, like Coates, Galois, Abel, Ramanujan, and Majorana, died in their youth. In these cases, we do not know how they may have fared had they lived past their prime.) In any event, he seems unable to sustain a constant and a continuous ascent. Why is this the case? I shall not attempt to answer this question but pass on to some more concrete considerations.

The question to which I now wish to address myself is how one may evaluate scientific theories as works of art in the manner of literary or art criticism. The case of the general theory of relativity provides a good example, since almost everyone is agreed that it is a beautiful theory. I think it is useful to inquire wherein the source of this beauty lies. It will not do, I think, to dismiss such an inquiry with an assertion such as Dirac's (made in a different context):

> [Mathematical beauty] cannot be defined any more than beauty in art can be defined, but which people who study mathematics usually have no difficulty in appreciating.

Nor do I think that one should be satisfied with a remark such as Born's:

> It [the general theory of relativity] appeared to me like a great work of art, to be enjoyed and admired from a distance.

(Parenthetically, may I say, quite frankly, that I do not know what to make of Born's remark. Has the general theory of relativity to be admired only from a distance? Does it not require study and development like any other branch of the physical sciences?)

In spite of the inherent difficulties which beset such discussions, I shall attempt to clarify why the general theory of relativity appeals to our aesthetic sense and why we consider it as beautiful. For this purpose, it is necessary to adopt some criteria for beauty. I shall adopt two.

The first is the criterion of Francis Bacon:

> There is no excellent beauty that hath not some strangeness in the proportion!

(Strangeness, in this context, has the meaning "exceptional to a degree that excites wonderment and surprise.")

The second criterion, as formulated by Heisenberg, is complementary to Bacon's:

> Beauty is the proper conformity of the parts to one another and to the whole.

That the general theory of relativity has some strangeness in the proportion, in the Baconian sense, is manifest. It consists primarily in relating, in juxtaposition, two fundamental concepts which had, till then, been considered as entirely independent: the concepts of space and time, on the one hand, and the concepts of matter and motion, on the other. Indeed, as Pauli wrote in 1919, "The geometry of space-time is not given; it is determined by matter and its motion." In the fusion of gravity and metric that followed, Einstein accomplished in 1915 what Riemann had prophesied in 1854, namely, that the metric field must be causally connected with matter and its motion.

Perhaps the greatest strangeness in the proportion consists in our altered view of space-time. As Eddington wrote: "Space is not a lot of points close together; it is a lot of distances interlocked."

There is another aspect of Einstein's founding of his general theory of relativity that continues to be a marvel. It is this: We can readily concede that Newton's laws of gravitation require to be modified to allow for the finiteness of the velocity of light and to disallow instantaneous action at a distance. With this concession, it follows that the deviations of the planetary orbits from the Newtonian predictions must be quadratic in v/c where v is a measure of the velocity of the planet in its orbit and c is the velocity of light. In planetary systems, these deviations, even in the most favorable cases, can amount to no more than a few parts in a million. Accordingly, it would have been entirely sufficient if Einstein had sought a theory that would allow for such small deviations from the predictions of the Newtonian theory by a perturbative treatment. That would have been the normal way. But that was not Einstein's way: he sought, instead, for an exact theory. And he arrived at his field equations by qualitative arguments of a physical nature combined with an unerring sense for mathematical elegance and simplicity. The fact that Einstein was able to arrive at a complete physical theory by such speculative thought is the reason why, when we follow his thoughts, we feel "as if a wall which separated us from truth has collapsed" (Weyl).

The foregoing remarks apply only to the foundations of the theory leading to the field equations. We must now ask whether, on further examination, the theory satisfies the second criterion for beauty, namely, "the conformity of the parts to one another, and to the whole." The theory most abundantly satisfies this criterion while revealing at every stage a "strangeness in the proportion." Let me give a few illustrations.

Consider, first, the solutions which the general theory of relativity allows for black holes. As is known, black holes partition the three-dimensional space into two regions: an inner region, bounded by a smooth two-dimensional null-surface, which (the inner region) is incommunicable to the outer region which is, in turn, asymptotically flat. It is a startling fact that with these very simple and necessary restrictions, the general theory allows for stationary black holes a single unique two-parameter family of solutions. This is the Kerr family in which the two parameters are the mass and the angular momentum of the black hole. What is even more remarkable, the metric for this family of solutions is explicitly known. The Kerr metric is axisymmetric and represents a black hole rotating about the axis of symmetry.

The axisymmetric character of the Kerr geometry clearly guarantees that the energy of a test particle describing a geodesic, as well as its component of the angular momentum about the axis of symmetry, will be conserved. In addition to these two conserved quantities, the Kerr geometry unexpectedly allows for the test particle a third conserved quantity (discovered by Brandon Carter). In consequence, the Hamilton-Jacobi equation, governing the motion of a test particle, is separable in its variables; and the solution of the geodesic equations can be reduced to quadratures. This was surprising enough. But what is even more surprising is that all the equations of mathematical physics—the scalar wave equation, Maxwell's equations, Dirac's equation, and the equations governing the propagation of gravitational waves—all, are separable in Kerr geometry (even as they are in Minkowskian geometry) and can, therefore, be solved explicitly.

One experiences similar astonishment when one realizes that the singularity theorems of Penrose and Hawking require that our universe must necessarily have originated in a singularity and that, in consequence, we are compelled to contemplate the nature of the physical processes that will occur at densities of the order of 10^{93}g/cm^3, in volumes with linear dimensions of the order of 10^{-33}cm, and in intervals of time of the order of 10^{-44} seconds—dimensions which must stagger even this audience.

Or again, Hawking's theorem that the surface area of a black hole must always increase suggests the identification of the surface area with the thermodynamic entropy of the black hole; and this leads to an intimate connection between thermodynamics, geometry, and gravity.

There is clearly no lack of strangeness in the proportion in all these!

Everything I have said so far is in conformity with the two criteria of beauty with which I started. But there is yet another aspect of the matter which remains to be considered.

When Henry Moore visited the University of Chicago some ten years ago, I had the occasion to ask him how one should view sculptures: from afar or from nearby. Moore's response was that the greatest sculptures can be viewed—indeed, should be viewed—from all distances since new aspects of beauty will be revealed in every scale. Moore cited the sculptures of Michelangelo as examples. In the same way, the general theory of relativity reveals strangeness in the proportion at any level in which one may explore its consequences. One illustration must suffice.

If one enlarges Einstein's equations to the Einstein-Maxwell equations, that is, the field equations appropriate for space pervaded by an electromagnetic field, and seeks spherically symmetric solutions, one obtains a solution describing a black hole with a mass and an electric charge. This solution was discovered by Reissner and by Nordström as a generalization of the well known solution of Schwarzschild. Because of the charge of the black hole, it is clear that if an electromagnetic wave is incident on the black hole, a certain fraction of the incident electromagnetic energy will be reflected back in the form of gravitational waves. Conversely, if a gravitational wave is incident on the black hole, a certain fraction of the incident gravitational energy will be reflected back in the form of electromagnetic waves. The remarkable fact is that the two fractions are identically the same, that is, for all frequencies. This result was not expected; the underlying cause for it has now been traced to the time-reversibility of the (classical) laws of physics. This example illustrates how strangeness in the proportion is revealed by the general theory of relativity at all levels of exploration. And it is this fact, more than any other, that contributes to the unparalleled beauty of the general theory of relativity.

So far, my remarks have been confined to what we may all concede as great ideas conceived by great minds. It does not, however, follow that beauty is experienced only in the context of great ideas and by great minds. This is no more true than that the joys of creativity are restricted to a fortunate few. They are, indeed, accessible to each one of us provided we are attuned to the perception of strangeness in the proportion and the conformity of the parts to one another and to the whole. And there is satisfaction also to be gained from harmoniously organizing a domain of science with order, pattern, and coherence. Examples of such organizations are Jacobi's *Vorlesungen über Dynamik,* Boltzmann's *Vorlesungen über Gas Theorie,* Sommerfeld's *Atombau und Spektrallinen,* Dirac's *Principles of Quantum Mechanics,* and the various gems of exposition which Schrödinger wrote in his later years. The translucence of the eternal splendor through material phenomena (of which Plotinus spoke) are made iridescent in these books.

May I conclude then by suggesting that each of us, in our own modest ways, can achieve satisfaction in our quest for beauty in science like the players in Virginia Woolf's *The Waves:*

> There is a square; there is an oblong. The players take the square and place it upon the oblong. They place it very accurately; they make a perfect dwelling place. Very little is left outside. The structure is now visible; what was inchoate is here stated; we are not so various or so mean; we have made oblongs and stood them upon squares. This is our triumph; this is our consolation.

5

Edward Arthur Milne: His Part in the Development of Modern Astrophysics

I

Milne entered the arena of astrophysics in 1921. At that time, only the barest beginnings had been made in what have since become the two main pillars of modern astrophysics: the theory of stellar atmospheres and the theory of stellar structure.

In 1920, there was only one extant book which may be considered as treating topics in theoretical astrophysics: Robert Emden's *Gas Kugeln*—or gas spheres—published in 1907. Emden's book gives a surprisingly complete account of gaseous masses in equilibrium under their own gravitation and in which the pressure is proportional to some power of the density. This is the theory of the polytropic gas spheres—a theory which was to play a key role in the subsequent investigations of Eddington and of Milne. Emden's book, besides its more well-known parts dealing with polytropic gas spheres, includes a discussion of the physical conditions in the solar atmosphere with an account, in fact, of Karl Schwarzschild's inferences of 1906 that the outer layers of the sun cannot be in convective equilibrium but rather in radiative equilibrium. Schwarzschild had drawn his inferences from the finite brightness of the solar limb—a matter to which I shall return presently. Another landmark of this same period is a paper by Arthur Schuster in 1905 in which a problem in the theory of radiative transfer, relevant to the formation of absorption lines in the solar and in stellar atmospheres, is treated.

This Milne Lecture was given at Oxford University on 6 December 1979. It was published in the *Quarterly Journal of the Royal Astronomical Society* 21 (1980): 93–107, and is reprinted here with permission.

The concept of radiative equilibrium was further analyzed by Schwarzschild in 1914. In 1916, Eddington introduced these same concepts in the larger context of the equilibrium of the stars as a whole and had begun the first of his celebrated series of papers dealing with the internal constitution of the stars; and in 1918, Eddington formulated his pulsation theory of stellar variability.

Atomic theory was still very much in its infancy; and Saha's papers dealing with the ionization and excitation of atomic species, at the temperatures and pressures to be expected in stellar atmospheres, were yet to appear.

This was the time when Milne entered the arena of astrophysics. Let me say at once that, more than the particular advances for which he was responsible, his greater contribution was his attitude and his style. I shall say more about them later.

II

It was fortunate that the problem to which Milne first turned his attention was one that suited his style and his methods admirably. As I shall indicate presently, the results which he derived in these, his first and earliest investigations in astrophysics, have remained essentially unchanged over the years and have provided the basis for certain permanent features of our understanding of the outer layers of the stars. For this reason, I shall consider them in some detail.

The problem which Milne considered was concerned with the interpretation of the variation of the brightness of the sun across its disc. This is the phenomenon of the darkening of the sun towards the limb illustrated in figure 1. This variation of the brightness across the solar disc occurs not only in the total brightness but also in the different wavelengths or colors.

It is clear from figure 2 that the darkening towards the limb is simply an expression of the angular dependence of the intensity of the emergent radiation. This problem of the darkening of the sun towards the limb had been considered by Karl Schwarzschild in 1906, and he had related it to the prevalence of radiative equilibrium and to the resulting variation of temperature in the outer layers of the sun. The interpretation of the darkening, on the basis of these ideas, is very simple.

The basic fact is that the radiation from all depths contributes to the emergent radiation; only the radiation from the deeper layers is increasingly attenuated by the opacity (i.e., the fogginess) of the overlaying material. On this account, we may say that the radiation which emerges from the surface is characteristic of the radiation prevailing at

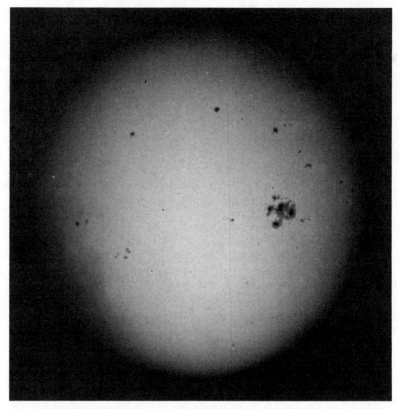

Fig. 1 Photograph illustrating the darkening of the sun towards the limb. Courtesy of Yerkes Observatory.

a certain average depth below the surface. We may, in fact, say that there is a depth to which we effectively see. This depth, measured by the extent to which the overlaying layers attenuate the radiation traversing them, must be the same for all wavelengths and for all angles of emergence. In other words, we effectively see down to an optical depth of unity in all cases. (Radiation traversing material of optical depth unity will be attenuated by a factor of approximately 1/4.)

Since radiation emerging at an angle traverses a path which is slanting through the atmosphere, it is clear that such radiation will be representative of the radiation prevailing at a level not as deep as the level which is representative of the radiation which emerges normally from the surface. Since we should expect the deeper layers to be at higher temperatures, it follows that the radiation emerging at an angle will be characteristic of a temperature lower than the temperature character-

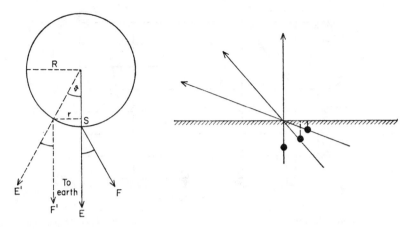

FIG. 2 Illustrating the fact that the darkening results from the angular dependence of the emergent radiation and on the temperature gradient in the atmosphere.

istic of the radiation emerging normally. Therefore, the intensity of the radiation emerging at an angle must be less than that emerging normally (see fig. 2). In other words, there must be a darkening towards the limb.

From the foregoing description, it is clear that the principal problem, which requires solution before we can account for the phenomenon of darkening, is the distribution of the temperature in the outer layers. Once the temperature distribution has been ascertained, the emergent intensity at any given angle can be directly related to the variation of the opacity (i.e., the absorption coefficient or the absorptive power) of the material for light of different wavelengths.

Suppose $\bar{\kappa}$ is some mean absorption coefficient and let τ be the optical depths measured in terms of $\bar{\kappa}$. Let T_τ be the temperature that prevails at depth τ. Then at the depth τ, the spectral distribution of the radiation will be determined by the Planck distribution

$$B_\nu(T_\tau) = \frac{2h\nu^3}{c^2} \frac{1}{\exp(h\nu/k\,T_\tau) - 1},\qquad(1)$$

where ν, c, and h denote the frequency, the velocity of light, and Planck's constant, respectively. Accordingly, the intensity of the emergent radiation, at an angle θ to the normal and with a frequency ν, will be given by

$$I_\nu(\theta) = \int_0^\infty d\tau\, B_\nu(T_\tau)\left(\frac{\kappa_\nu}{\bar{\kappa}}\right)\exp[-(\kappa_\nu/\bar{\kappa})\,\tau\sec\theta]\sec\theta,\qquad(2)$$

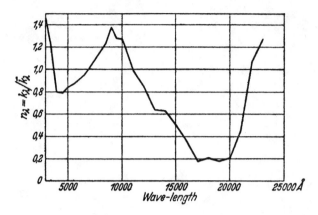

FIG. 3 Milne's deduced variation of the solar continuous absorption coefficient with wavelength.

where κ_ν is the absorption coefficient at the particular frequency considered.

It is clear that from a comparison of the observed intensities with those which would follow from equation (2), we can deduce the variation of the absorption coefficient with wavelength (as determined by $\kappa_\nu/\bar{\kappa}$); and this variation will clearly determine something significant about the constitution of the solar atmosphere.

The problem, which I have outlined, was solved by Milne with exceptional thoroughness in his early papers; and he deduced from the solar observations the variation of the solar continuous absorption-coefficient with the wavelength. His results are shown in figure 3.

Milne emphasized two features of the deduced variation: first, that the absorption coefficient increases gradually over the entire visual part of the spectrum and attains a very well-defined maximum at about 8000 Å; and second, that beyond 8000 Å it decreases to a very deep minimum at about 16,000 Å.

Milne's analysis was repeated by others, in other forms, during the following decades; they all confirmed his major deductions. I shall consider one such confirmation taken from an investigation of Chalonge and Kourganoff in 1946 (some twenty-five years after Milne).

Consider a level at some assigned temperature T and ask for the opacity of the overlaying layers in various wavelengths. Clearly, this question can be answered with the aid of Milne's basic theory. The results of the analysis of Chalonge and Kourganoff are exhibited in figure 4. The basic deductions of Milne are clearly confirmed.

The simplicity of the analysis leading to the deduced variation of the continuous absorption coefficient with wavelength signifies, un-

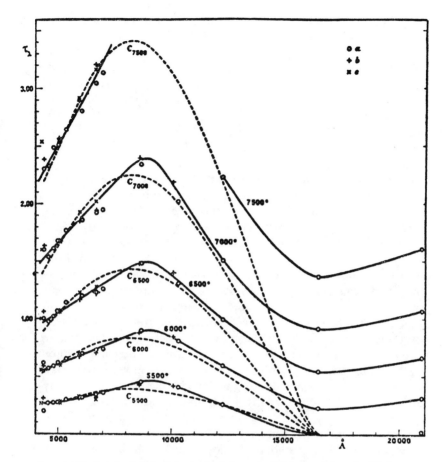

FIG. 4 Optical depth (τ_λ) of photospheric layers at different wavelengths (Chalonge and Kourganoff 1946). Dotted lines are H⁻ absorption; right part of graph explained by free-free transitions.

equivocally, that a fundamental constituent of the solar atmosphere is here involved. As to what this constituent may be finally emerged only during the forties with the definite isolation of what could then be truly described as a new fundamental constituent of the solar atmosphere.

Let me briefly trace the history of these developments since it represents the fruition of Milne's basic and earliest researches.

By an application of the variational method by which one can set upper bounds to the ground-state energies of atomic systems, Hylleraas and Bethe independently showed in 1930 that a hydrogen atom can stably bind itself to an electron to form a negative ion with a binding energy exceeding 3/4 eV. But it was only in 1938 that Rupert Wildt, returning to the fundamental problem that had been posed by Milne sixteen years earlier and which had been sidestepped during the intervening years, pointed out that the negative ions of hydrogen must be present in substantial concentration in the solar atmosphere if hydrogen is indeed as abundant as other evidences had indicated. This was a most fruitful suggestion; it represented a key discovery which made possible all later developments in the theory of stellar atmospheres. But several difficulties had to be overcome before a definitive identification of the negative ion of hydrogen as the source of the continuous absorption in the solar atmosphere could be made.

The principal difficulty was the theoretical determination of the continuous absorption coefficient of the negative ion of hydrogen. This is neither the place nor the occasion to go into the history of the solution of this problem. For those who might be interested, I may refer to a comprehensive account that has recently been published by Sir David Bates in *Physics Reports*. Figure 5 (taken from Bates's report) suffices to show the years of effort that were required to resolve this problem. It is manifest from this figure that a quantally reliable evaluation of the continuous absorption coefficient of the negative hydrogen-ion reproduces the essential features of the curve deduced by Milne in 1922 (see also fig. 4). And it should not be overlooked that at the time this identification was made, the negative ion of hydrogen was a theoretically predicted atomic species; the confirmation of the theoretically predicted continuum by laboratory experiments was still ten years in the future.

So we come to the end of one major chapter in the history of modern theoretical astrophysics which began with Milne's researches.

III

I now turn to a second chapter. At about the time Milne was working on the problem of the continuous spectrum of the sun, R. H. Fowler and C. G. Darwin were developing their new approach to statistical mechanics, and Saha's first successful quantitative applications of the theory of statistical (or rather, in his case, thermodynamic) equilibrium of stellar reversing layers were appearing in a series of papers in the *Philosophical Magazine* and in the *Proceedings of the Royal Society*.

Saha's theory was based on the following observation: An atmosphere absorbs a different optical spectrum for each stationary stage of ionization, and in fact a different set of lines for each stationary state belonging to each stage; therefore the relative intensities of the absorp-

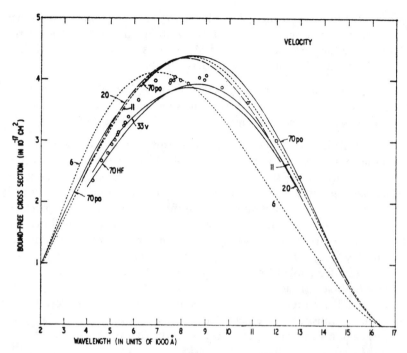

FIG. 5   Photo-detachment cross-section of H⁻. Experimental values due to Smith
and Burch (1959). Number of variational parameters in bound-state wave-function is
indicated on each curve. Broken lines used if ejected electron is represented by plane
wave: 6 (Williamson 1943), 11 (Henrich 1944), 20 (Chandrasekhar 1953). Full lines
used if ejected electron is represented by more refined approximation: 70 po, polarized
orbital, Bell and Kingston (1967); 70 HF, Hartree-Fock expansion, Doughty et al.
(1967); 33v, variational, determined by simplified Kohn-Feshbach method, together
with Rotenberg-Stein bound function, Ajmera and Chung (1975). All calculations
based on the matrix element of the velocity (Chandrasekhar 1945). (From D. R. Bates,
"Other Men's Flowers," *Physics Reports* **35**, 306 [1978])

tion lines of its successive spectra in the spectrum of any star must
give some indication of the relative number of atoms in the various
stages of ionization in the reversing layer and therefore of the temperature and the pressure. Saha's early application of this idea was based
on the points of first and last "marginal" appearances of particular
spectral lines. At such points, Saha had argued that the fraction of the
atoms in the reversing layer capable of absorbing the line must be very
small. And if the corresponding pressure could be estimated, the temperature can be deduced.

The precision of these early calculations was questionable owing to
the difficulty of formulating conditions for the marginal appearance of
particular lines: we do not know how small the "very small" fraction

of atoms must be at marginal appearance; also, the point of marginal appearance will depend on the relative abundance of the element responsible for the line. Fowler and Milne in a series of papers published during 1923–25 reformulated the basic problem as follows:

> Other things being equal, the intensity of a given absorption line in a stellar spectrum varies always in the same sense as the concentration of the atoms in the reversing layer capable of absorbing the line.

The difficulties with the concept of marginal appearance are avoided in this formulation, and Fowler and Milne first devoted their attention to the place in the stellar sequence at which a given line attains its *maximum intensity*. On the stated premise, the maximum intensity will be attained at the maximum concentration of the atoms capable of absorbing the line; and the conditions for this to happen will involve only the temperature and the pressure. In other words, the temperature at which, for a given pressure, a given line attains its maximum is simply deducible from the properties of the equilibrium state. This was the first satisfactory way of applying Saha's theory quantitatively to fix stellar temperatures and pressures. In this manner, Fowler and Milne established a theoretical temperature-scale for the grand sequence of the Harvard spectral types for the first time: a true landmark in theoretical astrophysics.

In subsequent papers, Milne showed that the concepts of mean pressure and mean temperature, that are at the base of his studies with Fowler, in turn require refinements in at least two directions. First, we must make precise the meaning we are to attach to a phrase such as "the intensity of an absorption line." And second, we must allow for the variation of the temperature, the pressure, and the various attendant physical parameters through the layers in which the absorption line is formed. We must, in fact, construct model stellar atmospheres. While Milne formulated some of the basic considerations which must be incorporated in such refinements, he did not pursue them in any great depth or detail. They were left for Pannekoek, Unsold, Minnaert, and a host of others to analyze and to complete. The construction of model stellar atmospheres has now become a large industry, but it had its beginnings in the heroic efforts of Saha, Fowler, and Milne towards a basic physical understanding.

IV

I now turn to Milne's work bearing on stellar structure. Already during the years Milne was occupied with problems in the theory of stellar atmospheres, he was turning his attention to problems in the theory of stellar structure. Thus, in a paper published in 1923, he considered the effect of a slow rotation on Eddington's standard model for the stars and on his mass-luminosity relation. This is an altogether exemplary paper in which the mathematics and the physics are scored in counterpoint. (Perhaps I may be allowed to state here, parenthetically, that it was this paper of Milne's which stimulated me to develop a complete theory of distorted polytropes some ten years later.)

But it was only in 1929 that Milne seriously turned his attention to problems in the theory of stellar structure; but it was begun inauspiciously under the pressure of a bitter controversy with Eddington. This controversy was an unhappy episode which, at least in my judgment, had tragic repercussions on Milne's subsequent work. I shall not say anything more about this episode on this occasion, but it is not possible to avoid overtones of it in any account of Milne's work after 1929.

In 1926, R. H. Fowler had shown in a fundamental paper that the state of matter in the interiors of the white-dwarf stars, such as the companion of Sirius, cannot be a perfect gas governed by the equation of state, $p = \Re \rho T$ (where p denotes the pressure, ρ the density, T the temperature, and $\Re$ the gas constant); and that it should be governed by the equation of state provided by the then-new statistical mechanics of Fermi and Dirac and, indeed, in its limiting form when all the energy levels of the free electrons below a certain threshold are occupied and none above it. In other words, matter must be "degenerate."

Fowler's discussion convincingly demonstrated that Eddington's assumption that the stars are wholly gaseous, with the normal equation of state, cannot be universally valid: the white dwarfs are examples to the contrary. In the white dwarfs, the matter is degenerate and the relation between the pressure and the density is, in a good approximation, independent of the temperature. It is therefore legitimate and proper to inquire when and under what circumstances degeneracy can develop in the interior of the stars. But Milne's inquiry was not so directed. He started with the premise—at least, he took it as a foregone conclusion—that all stars *must* have domains of degeneracy and that they *must* belong to one or the other of two classes which he called centrally condensed configurations and collapsed configurations, the distinction between them consisting mainly in the extent of the domains of degeneracy.

In his first detailed paper on the subject, published in January 1931, Milne developed some powerful analytical tools for constructing composite stellar configurations in which different relations between pressure and density obtain in different parts. Besides, Milne stimulated his long-time friend R. H. Fowler to undertake a systematic study of *all* the solutions of Emden's differential equation governing polytropic distributions.

(Parenthetically, may I quote here some remarks of G. H. Hardy's at a meeting of the Royal Astronomical Society in January 1931? Hardy, as some of you may remember, was the Savillian Professor of Geometry here in Oxford during the twenties. He said (with his tongue in his cheek, as he confessed to me later):

> As a mathematician, I don't care two straws what the stars are really like. . . . But I am particularly interested in Mr. Fowler's paper. . . . His paper is probably the only one of the collection which is of lasting value, for he is certainly right, whereas it is extremely likely that everyone else will be shown to be wrong.

I am afraid that what Hardy prophesied has mostly come to pass.)

To return to Milne's investigations: It was pointed out to him, even before he had communicated his first paper to the Royal Astronomical Society, that the mass of a wholly degenerate star cannot exceed a certain limiting value; and that this fact in turn places an upper limit to the mass that can be contained in the degenerate cores of stars; and finally, that in view of the increasing importance of the radiation pressure in massive stars, sufficiently massive stars cannot possibly develop domains of degeneracy. But Milne would not accept these conclusions. Instead, he wrote:

> If the consequences of quantum mechanics contradict very obvious much more immediate considerations, then something must be wrong either with the principles underlying the equation-of-state-derivation or with the aforementioned general principles. Kelvin's gravitational-age-of-the-Sun calculation was perfectly sound; but it contradicted other considerations which had not then been realized. To me it is clear that matter cannot behave as you predict. . . . Your marshalling of authorities such as Bohr, Pauli, Fowler, Wilson, etc., very impressive as it is, leaves me cold.

From the vantage point of today, it is clear that Milne's negative attitude prevented him from realizing that the incorporation, positively, of the consequences of Fermi degeneracy, leads one directly to conclude that massive stars, after they have exhausted their sources of energy, must collapse to black holes—a conclusion which Eddington drew but which neither Eddington nor Milne would accept. This failure on their part illustrates the danger of perceiving Nature in the images of one's personal beliefs and faiths.

As I said earlier, in the course of his analysis, Milne developed powerful analytical methods for treating composite stellar models. His methods were ideally suited for exploring stellar models with degenerate cores of the kind that stars can have consistently with their allowed upper limit. Milne could easily have carried out such explorations. That he did not was unfortunate both for Milne and for astrophysics.

V

Before I turn to Milne's last and largest phase of his work, namely, kinematic relativity and cosmology, I should like to make a reference—if only a brief one—to a beautiful analysis in stellar kinematics which he published in 1935. In this paper, Milne analyzed the differential motions that can occur in a stellar system, in the manner Stokes had analyzed hydrodynamic fluid-motion into three parts: a rotation, a sheer, and an expansion. From the point of view of this analysis, the occurrence of the so-called double-sine wave, in the variation, with the galactic longitude, of the radial velocities of stars with an amplitude proportional to the distance of the stars, becomes self-evident. Milne's analysis provided the base for much dynamical discussion carried out subsequently.

VI

I now come to a phase of Milne's work which he undoubtedly considered as his most important scientific contribution. Thus, referring to his theory of the expanding universe, he wrote to me in a letter dated 6 July 1943:

> I do not know whether I have ever opened my heart to you on that theory. I only know that the texture of the argumentation in it is something utterly and surprisingly different from usual mathematical physics, and that when it comes to be recognized, it will be regarded as revolutionary. It is not usual to crack up one's own work in this way; but it is all very near my heart.

Perhaps it is not fair that I quote what Milne clearly meant only for me. But to the extent that, in my assessment, I am unable to give to his theory the same exalted place, it is necessary that I acknowledge it with equal frankness.

In developing his kinematic theory of relativity, Milne took the strong position that a theory of gravitation can do very well without the general theory of relativity. Indeed, *Gravitation without Relativity* is the title of a contribution which he wrote for a collection of essays that was presented to Einstein in 1949 and which was included in volume

7 of the *Library of Living Philosophies—Albert Einstein, Philosopher-Scientist* (edited by Paul A. Schilpp). Einstein's reaction to Milne's contribution, in his concluding essay in the volume, was:

> Concerning Milne's ingenious reflections, I can only say that I find their theoretical basis too narrow. From my point of view one cannot arrive, by way of theory, at any at least somewhat reliable results in the field of cosmology, if one makes no use of the principle of general relativity.

In juxtaposition with this view of Einstein's, let me place Milne's view of the general theory of relativity:

> Einstein's law of gravitation is by no means an inevitable consequence of the conceptual basis given by describing phenomena by means of a Riemannian metric. I have never been convinced of its necessity. . . . General relativity is like a garden where flowers and weeds grow together. The useless weeds are cut with the desired flowers and separated later!

And Milne goes on to say, "In our garden we grow only flowers."

To be complete, I may be allowed to state my own view. General relativity proceeds on the assumption that a theory of gravitation must reduce to all of the Newtonian laws as they operate in the "small" as, for example, in determining the motions as they obtain in the solar system; and that only a theory constructed, consistently with the other laws of physics (as incorporated in the principle of equivalence) can, with confidence, be extended to the larger context of the universe. Milne's procedure is exactly the converse of this. He proceeds on the assumption that gravitation can be understood by first constructing a theory of the universe in the large and then descending to phenomena manifested in the small. Apart from the fact that Milne did not succeed in completing his program, it is probable that the program is an inherently impossible one.

Well! There you have three views of varying authority!

Having stated my overall negative view of this phase of Milne's work, let me say at once that there are some key aspects of his work which are refreshingly original. Thus, Milne's analysis of Lorentz transformations in terms of light signals exchanged by observers is a model of precision and economy of thought. It deserves much wider knowledge than it enjoys. As Bondi has written:

> I feel that not nearly enough has been said about the deep debt of gratitude that we owe to Milne, who in his work on cosmology, introduced the notion of the radar method of measuring distance.

I now turn to the ideas which Milne contributed to cosmology and which have secured for themselves permanent places in the current literature.

During the late twenties and early thirties, the facts which were perceived as basic for a theory of the universe as a whole were the following:

1. In a first approximation, the distribution of the extragalactic nebulae is locally homogeneous and isotropic.

and

2. The galaxies are receding from us and from one another with velocities which are proportional to their mutual distances, as codified in Hubble's law.

The discussion of these facts in the framework of the relativistic cosmological models of Friedmann and Lemaître, as popularized particularly by Eddington, gave one the impression—intended or not—that general relativity is necessary to incorporate them into a coherent theory. But this perception exaggerated the role of general relativity. And Milne was certainly correct in pointing out that the facts considered have a simple interpretation which requires no special appeal to any particular theory.

The observed expansion of the universe and the Hubble relation imply, only, that all the nebulae we now observe must have been, at one time, close together in a small volume of space. Suppose, then, that at some initial time, t_0, the nebulae were all confined to a small volume (see fig. 6), and that they all had the same speed V but in random directions. Then, after a sufficient length of time $(t-t_0)$, these same nebulae will have moved outward and will be confined to a relatively thin spherical shell of radius $V (t-t_0)$. Now, suppose that, in addition to the nebulae with the velocity V, the same initial small volume had also contained nebulae with half the velocity V. Then, after a lapse of time $(t-t_0)$, these nebulae will be confined to a thin spherical shell of half the radius $\frac{1}{2} V (t-t_0)$. More generally, it is clear that if the original volume had contained nebulae of all velocities, then after a sufficient length of time, the nebulae, with differing velocities, will become segregated; they will, in fact, arrange themselves at distances from the center which are proportional to their distances in conformity with Hubble's law. Or, as Milne stated: "the birds of a feather flock together."

This simple model we have described suggests that the observed expansion of the universe is simply the result of an early beginning of high mean density—a conclusion no one denies at the present time.

Again, as Milne emphasized, a homogeneous swarm of particles receding from a chosen particle in it with velocities proportional to

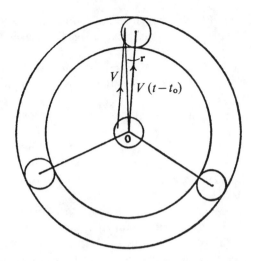

FIG. 6   Illustrating the emergence of a Hubble relation for a system initially confined to a small volume.

their distances from it, has a remarkable property. As a simple application of the parallelogram of velocities shows (see fig. 7), the description of the motions will be the same with respect to any other particle in the swarm provided one does not go too near the boundary. In such a system, each particle in the swarm can consider itself as at the center of the swarm with the other particles receding from it radially with velocities proportional to their distances from it, with the same constant of proportionality. In other words, a universe which is homogeneous and isotropic and in which the motions satisfy a Hubble relation are related facts which derive their common origin in the requirement that the description of the universe is the same as viewed from all galaxies. This last requirement was formulated by Milne as a *cosmological principle*. Milne considered this principle as inviolable: it is the centerpiece of his kinematical theory of relativity.

For reasons I have already stated, I shall not go into any detailed assessment of Milne's kinematical theory of relativity. However, I shall indicate, following Milne's ideas, how the cosmological principle together with Newtonian laws can be used to derive a description of the universe locally adequate and which is in agreement with the relativistic models of Friedmann.

It is clear that the cosmological principle requires that the world-view of any observer, relative to himself, must have spherical symmetry about himself. Then, according to a theorem which is valid equally in the frameworks of the Newtonian theory and the theory of

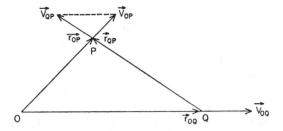

FIG. 7 Illustrating the fact that a cosmological principle is satisfied in a system in which velocity is proportional to distance. Particles P and Q are receding from point O at velocities proportional to their distance from O, but to an observer moving with particle Q, the only apparent motion of particle P is a recession from Q with a velocity proportional to the distance between P and Q.

general relativity, a particle at the boundary of a sphere, in a distribution of matter having spherical symmetry about the origin, will be gravitationally acted upon only by the matter interior to the sphere. Consequently, so long as the velocities of expansion are small compared to the velocity of light and the contribution of the pressure to the inertia can be neglected, we can restrict ourselves to the Newtonian laws of gravitation and to Newtonian concepts in analyzing the dynamics of the motions in the system. And we should expect that the results so derived will be valid also in the wider framework of general relativity, within the stated limitations. Indeed, as Milne and, more fully, Milne and McCrea showed, the equations which follow from the Newtonian analysis are in agreement with those which follow from a relativistic analysis, again, within the stated limitations. But one must go to the general theory of relativity if the limitations imposed, by ignoring the inertial effects of the pressure and by disallowing velocities comparable to that of light, are to be avoided.

I am doubtful if Milne would have approved of my presentation of his ideas or would have allowed the concession to general relativity that I have made. Nevertheless, the theory as I have described it, following in main Milne's ideas, is a part of what every student of cosmology now learns.

VII

Let me conclude by describing in general terms what manner of a scientist Milne was.

Milne's special strength was in reducing a complex problem to its elements and analyzing each element as to its content and as to its meaning. The crisp and vigorous style of his writings are manifestations of his keen analytic intellect. He once told me that often his pen could hardly keep pace with the flow of his ideas. Besides, he took delight in solving his analytical problems with grace and elegance. These admirable traits are discernible in all of his writings, though in much of his later writings they are shrouded, to a larger or smaller extent, by elements of self-defense and controversy. But when the air was free and his thoughts were untrammeled, his obvious enjoyment, in the flow of his ideas and in the course and texture of his arguments, transports the reader to an equal measure of enjoyment. Nowhere is this transmission of joy more sustained than in his marvellous book on *Vectorial Mechanics*. One can also experience the same delight in some of his papers which were not in the main stream of his scientific concerns; these gems, in many ways, reveal Milne at his best.

If I were asked to select a paper of Milne's which illustrates his originality, his style, and, above all, his sheer delight in what he is doing, I should select his paper on "The Energetics of Non-Steady States, with Applications to Cepheid Variation" published in the *Oxford Quarterly* in 1933. (But even this paper is marred by some unnecessary elements of controversy.) Milne formulated the ideas contained in this paper during the course of a conversation we were having in my rooms in Cambridge in 1933. Milne was wondering how the phenomenon of Cepheid variability could be grasped in a general theoretical framework without any reference to specific internal parameters such as pressure, temperature, etc. He said that a Cepheid variable is after all a heat engine; and recalling what he had learned from H. F. Newall about Griffith's heat engine, he rapidly developed a theoretical framework which led to the functional equation

$$(3) \qquad \kappa\phi(t) + \phi[t + b + \phi(t)] = 0,$$

for the time derivative of the relative amplitude of the light variation, where κ and b are certain constants.

Equation (3) has many remarkable properties. Thus, if ϕ takes the value zero at some instant of time, then it must take the value zero at an infinite succession of instants at intervals of time b apart. Further, if κ were unity, the solutions are periodic with a period $2b$; and a host of other intriguing properties.

At a later time, when Milne gave an account of this work at a meeting of the Royal Astronomical Society, he stated with undisguised delight that since the functional equation (3)

> gave periodic solutions reproducing some of the features of Cepheid light-curves . . . it should not be beyond the wit of man to devise an analysis [of Cepheid variability] which led to it!

In making an overall assessment of Milne, we have to remember that his early years in Cambridge were interrupted by World War I; that he contracted a fell disease in 1923 which was eventually to prove fatal in 1950; that there were personal tragedies of great magnitude in his life; that his scientific work was interrupted for long years by both World Wars; that during the last several years of his life, he was a sick man; and that, over and above all of these, there was his controversy with Eddington which embittered much of his scientific experience. When we remember all of these and remember also his many solid accomplishments, then we may in truth say, as his longtime friend and colleague Harry Plaskett said, "he died, as he lived, undefeated."

Eddington by Augustus John. Reproduced by permission of the Master and Fellows of Trinity College, Cambridge.

6

Eddington: The Most Distinguished Astrophysicist of His Time

I

When Eddington died in November 1944 at the age of sixty-two, Henry Norris Russell, his great contemporary across the Atlantic, wrote, "The death of Sir Arthur Eddington deprives astrophysics of its most distinguished representative."[1] I have taken my cue from Russell for the substance of this, the first of my two lectures.

Before I turn to an assessment of Eddington's contributions to astronomy and to astrophysics, I should like to start with a few biographical notes which may give some impression of the manner of man he was.

Arthur Stanley Eddington was born on 20 December 1882 at Kendal in Westmoreland. His father, Arthur Henry Eddington, was Headmaster and Proprietor of Stramongate School at Kendal where John Dalton had taught a century earlier. Forty-eight years later, when Eddington was conferred the Freedom of the Borough of Kendal, he recalled to say:

> The traditions of Kendal have been woven into my earliest memories
> as the home of the brief married life of my parents. I cannot but feel
> thankful that Kendal has recognised scientific work as a public service

These Centenary Lectures in Memory of Arthur Stanley Eddington were given in Cambridge under the auspices of Trinity College on 19 and 21 October 1982. They were published by the Cambridge University Press in 1983, and are reprinted here with the permission of the Cambridge University and of the Master and fellows of Trinity College.

of the utmost importance, not in any material sense; but that it has contributed something to the community. Kendal has an earlier association with science, that great chemist, perhaps the greatest of all chemists, who was Headmaster of Stramongate School, the same School of which a century later my father became Headmaster and where I was born. From John Dalton we had the atom. Now I have become an atom chaser myself. John Dalton must have left some germ behind him which lingered in the walls of Stramongate. I like to think of that continuity, and I am proud to have been able in a way to follow in the path which has been opened out by Kendal's great scientist.[2]

Eddington's father died in 1884; and his mother, together with her two young children, Stanley and his elder sister by four years, Winifred, moved to Weston-super-Mare. Here Eddington showed, quite early, his fascination with large numbers: he learnt the 24 × 24 multiplication table; and on one occasion started counting all the words in the Bible. Eddington never lost his fascination with large numbers. In later life, he often chose to write astronomical measures and distances with all their zeros explicitly. Thus, Eddington began an Evening Discourse to the British Association in Oxford in 1926 with:

> The stars are of remarkably uniform mass, that of the sun is—I will write it on the blackboard:
>
> 2 000 000 000 000 000 000 000 000 000 tons.
>
> I hope I have counted the 0's rightly, though I dare say you would not mind if there were one or two too many or too few. But nature *does* mind.[3]

And in 1935, when Eddington's interests had turned to the astronomical universe in the large, he introduced the subject with:[4]

	MILES
Distance of sun	93,000,000
Limit of solar system (Orbit of Pluto)	3,600,000,000
Distance of nearest star	25,000,000,000,000
Distance of nearest galaxy	6,000,000,000,000,000,000
Original circumference of the universe	40,000,000,000,000,000,000,000

With respect to large numbers, the most famous, of course, is the opening sentence of chapter 11 of his *Philosophy of Physical Science* published in 1939:

> I believe there are 15 747 724 136 275 002 577 605 653 961 181 555 468 044 717 914 527 116 709 366 231 425 076 185 631 031 296 protons in the universe, and the same number of electrons.[5]

This number, which is 136×2^{256}, has come to be known as Eddington's number. Bertrand Russell asked Eddington if he had computed this number himself or if he had someone else do it for him. Eddington replied that he had done it himself during an Atlantic crossing!

At Weston-super-Mare, Eddington attended Brymelyn School between 1893 and 1898. I recall Eddington telling me that at school one of the games he played was to make up English sentences which were grammatically correct but which made no sense, in the manner of Lewis Carroll. An example he gave me was, "To stand by the hedge and sound like a turnip." In later life, Eddington was wont to introduce such sentences in his more serious writings to make a point. Thus, in his Swarthmore Lecture, *Science and the Unseen World*, we find, "Human personalities are not measurable by symbols any more than you can extract the square root of a sonnet."[6]

I shall not go into any further details of his early education except to say that he entered Owen's College, Manchester, in 1898 and remained there for four years. His teachers in Owen's College included Sir Arthur Schuster and Sir Horace Lamb. Eddington seems to have maintained a deep admiration for Lamb all through his life. Thus, during the early twenties, when Eddington had become one of the most well-known figures of British science, he is reported to have said: "While I know what it is to be treated something like a lion, I would rather like to become something of a Lamb."

After a distinguished career at Manchester, Eddington proceeded to Cambridge in 1903 on a minor entrance-scholarship which was later changed to a major scholarship. He was the Senior Wrangler in 1904; was awarded the Smith's prize in 1907; and was elected to a Fellowship in Trinity in the same year. In 1936, I had the occasion to sit next to Alfred North Whitehead at a dinner at Harvard University. Whitehead recalled that, as one of the electors in 1907, he had ensured the election of Eddington to the Fellowship in preference to another who had submitted a much more voluminous thesis. And Whitehead seemed proud to recall this fact.

In 1907, in the same year that he was elected to the Fellowship at Trinity, Eddington, at the invitation of Sir William Christie, the Astronomer Royal, joined the staff of the Greenwich Observatory as a Chief Assistant. He had held this position for five years when, in 1912, he was elected to the Plumian Chair in Cambridge as the successor to Sir George Darwin. And in 1914, at the death of Sir Robert Ball, Eddington became the Director of the Cambridge Observatory, as well. He held these positions with great distinction for the next thirty years. And in Cambridge he made his home, first with his mother and sister and later with his sister alone.

I shall conclude my biographical notes with some remarks on Eddington's general views and habits.

Eddington was a Quaker; and as a Quaker, he was a conscientious objector during the First World War. I shall have more to say about his conscientious objection to the War in my next lecture. Now, I shall refer only to his Swarthmore Lecture for 1929, *Science and the Unseen World*. In this lecture, Eddington expressed with transparent sincerity his views on religion, science, and life generally. Let me read a few paragraphs which seem to summarize his views:

> Religious creeds are a great obstacle to any full sympathy between the outlook of the scientist and the outlook which religion is so often supposed to require. . . . The spirit of seeking which animates us refuses to regard any kind of creed as its goal. It would be a shock to come across a university where it was the practice of the students to recite adherence to Newton's laws of motion, to Maxwell's equations and to the electromagnetic theory of light. We should not deplore it the less if our own pet theory happened to be included, or if the list were brought up to date every few years. We should say that the students cannot possibly realise the intention of scientific training if they are taught to look on these results as things to be recited and subscribed to. Science may fall short of its ideal, and although the peril scarcely takes this extreme form, it is not always easy, particularly in popular science, to maintain our stand against creed and dogma.
>
> Rejection of creed is not inconsistent with being possessed by a living belief. We have no creed in science, but we are not lukewarm in our beliefs. The belief is not that all the knowledge of the universe that we hold so enthusiastically will survive in the letter; but a sureness that we are on the road. If our so-called facts are changing shadows, they are shadows cast by the light of constant truth.
>
> There is a kind of sureness which is very different from cocksureness. [7]

On a lighter matter. It was well known among Eddington's friends that he greatly looked forward to his solitary cycling tours in the spring and in the fall. But, perhaps, only a few knew of the careful record he kept of them. Before I left Cambridge in December 1936, Eddington showed me a large Bartholomew Touring Map of England in which he had carefully traced out in black ink all the different routes he had taken over the years. He further told me that the map that he had spread out before us was the second one, that the first had been mutilated by his dog, and that he had to transcribe on a new map the many routes he had traced out on the earlier one!

Eddington also told me that, while he was a Chief Assistant at Greenwich, he and Sydney Chapman (another great cycling enthusiast) had devised a criterion for judging cycling records. The criterion was the largest number n such that one had cycled n or more miles on n different days. (At a later time, when I mentioned this criterion to Chapman, he had forgotten it; but he did remember that he and Eddington had often compared notes on their cycling tours.)

It is perhaps touching that in every letter that he wrote to me subsequently, he included his latest value of n. The following extracts are from two letters:

> My cycling n is still 75. I was rather unlucky this Easter as I did two rides, seventy-four and three-quarters miles, which do not count; I still need four more rides for the next quantum jump. However, I had marvellously fine weather and splendid country, chiefly South Wales . . .
>
> . . . tomorrow I have to put on weird costume—knee breeches and silk hose!—and get my Order from the King. (1938 July 4)
>
> n is now 77. I think it was 75 when you were here. It made the last jump a few days ago when I took an eighty mile ride in the fen country. I have not been able to go on a cycling tour since 1940 because it is impossible to rely on obtaining accommodations for the night; so my records advance slowly. (1943 September 2)

One last matter. Eddington was addicted to solving the crossword puzzles in *The Times* and in the *New Statesman and Nation*. He rarely took more than five minutes for a puzzle. On occasions, Eddington allowed me to watch him as he solved a puzzle; and I marveled at his quickness.

III

I now turn to an assessment of Eddington's contributions to astronomy and to astrophysics. At the time Eddington entered astronomy in 1906, a revolutionary discovery had been made by J. C. Kapteyn of Groningen. Kapteyn was a great pioneer in the study of stellar motions; and his discovery was the following.

It had been assumed till then that the motions of stars were entirely random, with no preferential direction, in a *local standard of rest*, i.e., one in which the mean velocities of the stars, in the neighborhood, is zero. And a basic problem in stellar motions, as revealed by the proper motions and the radial velocities of the stars, was to determine the *solar motion*, i.e., the sun's "peculiar velocity" in the standard of rest determined by the stars in the neighborhood of the sun.

One the assumption of the randomness of the velocities with no

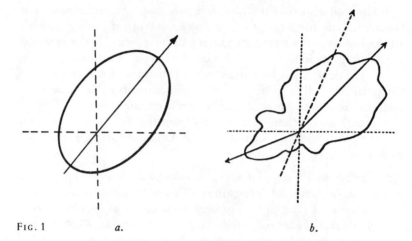

FIG. 1   *a.*   *b.*

direction preferentially distinguished, the distribution of the proper
motions, projected onto a small region of the sky, must have the appearance of an elongated ellipse (see fig. 1*a*). But this was not what
Kapteyn found. He found, instead, a double-lobed curve (see fig. 1*b*).
Eddington has described Kapteyn's discovery as follows.

> There is now a long series of "Groningen Publications" relating to
> these problems. The most interesting of them all is No. 6. But it is no
> use going to a library to consult it; for the interesting thing about No.
> 6 is that it was never written. Nature took an unexpected turn, and
> would not fit into the scheme which No. 6 was promised to elaborate.
> No. 5 was entitled "The distribution of cosmic velocities: Part I.
> Theory"; it was a study of how the motions of stars pursuing their
> courses at random would turn out statistically when the solar motion
> and effects of varying distance were allowed for. Meanwhile the ob-
> served Auwers-Bradley proper motions were being prepared for com-
> parison, so as to determine the numerical constants in the formulae. .But
> the theory, though it represented the unquestioned views of the time,
> turned out to be so wide of the mark that not even the beginnings of a
> comparison were possible; and the application of the formulae had to
> be abandoned. This was Kapteyn's great discovery of the two star
> streams, announced at the British Association meeting in South Africa
> in 1905, which revealed for the first time a kind of organization in the
> system of the stars and started a new era in the study of the relationships
> of these widely separated individuals.[8]

Eddington and Kapteyn interpreted this observed feature of the distribution of the proper motions of the stars by assuming that in the

FIG. 2   A. S. Eddington and J. C. Kapteyn.
The photograph reproduced in this figure is an enlargement of one taken by J. L.
Dreyer in Rome, May 1922, at the first meeting of the International Astronomical
Union after the First World War. The original was presented to the author by H. W.
Newton (formerly Chief Assistant at the Royal Greenwich Observatory) in November
1953.

neighborhood of the sun, the stars can be formally considered as belonging to two swarms—or, streams—in relative motion, and that the motions in each swarm, separately, are random. This is the Kapteyn-Eddington hypothesis of the *two star-streams*. Precisely, on this hypothesis, the assumption of a Maxwellian distribution of velocities that one had made earlier, namely,

$$(1) \qquad d\mathcal{N} = \mathcal{N} \frac{j^3}{\pi^{3/2}} e^{-j^2|u|^2} \, d\boldsymbol{u},$$

is replaced by,

$$(2) \qquad d\mathcal{N} = \mathcal{N}_1 \frac{j_1^3}{\pi^{1/2}} e^{-j_1^2|u-u_1|^2} \, d\boldsymbol{u} + \mathcal{N}_2 \frac{j_2^3}{\pi^{1/2}} e^{-j_2^2|u-u_2|^2} \, d\boldsymbol{u},$$

where $\mathcal{N}_1$ and $\mathcal{N}_2$ are the numbers of stars in the two streams, u_1 and u_2 are the velocities of the two streams in the local standard of rest, and j_1 and j_2 are the reciprocal mean speeds of the stars in the two streams, separately. Further the condition, that the distribution of the velocities (2) is with respect to the local standard of rest, requires that

$$(3) \qquad \mathcal{N}_1 \, u_1 + \mathcal{N}_2 \, u_2 = 0.$$

Eddington wrote several papers during his Greenwich years on the kinematics of the motions described by the distribution (2). He also developed analytic methods for determining the parameters, $\mathcal{N}_1$, $\mathcal{N}_2$, u_1, u_2, j_1, and j_2 of the two streams. And he determined them from the proper motions of the stars that were available to him. These papers of Eddington represent a remarkable synthesis of theory and observations; and they reveal his discriminating insight into the data of astronomical observations.

Adequate as the Kapteyn–Eddington hypothesis of the two star-streams was, an alternative interpretation of the same observations was given by Karl Schwarzschild. Schwarzschild's starting point was to replace the Maxwellian distribution (1) by the more general *ellipsoidal distribution*,

$$(4) \qquad d\mathcal{N} = \mathcal{N} \frac{j_1 j_2 j_3}{\pi^{3/2}} \, exp \, (-j_1^2 u_1^2 - j_2^2 u_2^2 - j_3^2 u_3^2) \, du_1 du_2 du_3,$$

in a suitably oriented frame of reference. Eddington has, himself, described Schwarzschild's alternative formulation as the most elegant and the most satisfying way of interpreting Kapteyn's discovery; and this interpretation has survived to this day.

This phase of Eddington's contributions came to an end with the publication in 1914 of his first book, *Stellar Movements and the Structure of the Universe.* This book, in large part, is devoted to a systematic presentation of the then extant knowledge of stellar motions. But the last chapter, "On the Dynamics of Stellar Systems", breaks new and fertile ground. After showing that binary stellar encounters cannot be effective in changing the directions of motions of the individual stars, Eddington concluded that the function $f(x, y, z, u, v, w, t)$ governing the distribution of the stars in the six-dimensional phase-space, must be determined by the dynamical orbits described by the stars in the smoothed-out gravitational potential of the whole system, i.e., by a solution of the six-dimensional Liouville equation (or the collisionless Boltzmann-equation as we would now call it).

In papers published in 1915 and 1916, Eddington sought solutions of Liouville's equation which are consistent with Schwarzschild's ellipsoidal distribution of velocities; and he obtained, in particular, a self-consistent solution appropriate for spherically symmetric stellar systems. In this same general context, Eddington pointed out, for the first time, how the virial theorem can be used to relate the average kinetic energy of a star in a cluster with its mean potential energy—a method which continues to be in vogue in the still larger context of galaxies and clusters of galaxies.

By these investigations, Eddington may be said to have founded the subject of stellar dynamics—a discipline which now stands on its own right.

IV

I now turn to what are, undoubtedly, Eddington's most significant contributions to the physical sciences: his founding of modern theoretical astrophysics and his creating the discipline of the structure, the constitution, and the evolution of the stars. His interest in the constitution of the stars was stimulated in 1916 by his efforts to understand the nature of Cepheid variability; and it culminated in 1926 with the publication of his *Internal Constitution of the Stars.* It should be remembered that during this same ten-year period, he was involved in the eclipse expeditions which provided the first verification of the deflection of light in its passage through a gravitational field—an event which he was later to describe as the most exciting event in his connection with astronomy—and in the writing of his *Mathematical Theory of Relativity* (1923) not to mention his *Report on the Relativity Theory of Gravitation* (1915) and his two popular books, *Space, Time, and Gravitation* (1920) and *Stars and Atoms* (1927)—a ten-year period of remarkable productivity.

In the domain of the internal constitution of the stars, Eddington recognized and established the following basic elements of our present understanding:

1. Radiation pressure must play an increasingly important role in maintaining the equilibrium of stars of increasing mass.

2. In parts of the star in which radiative equilibrium, as distinct from convective equilibrium, obtains, the temperature gradient is determined jointly by the distribution of the energy sources and of the opacity of the matter to the prevailing radiation field. Precisely,

$$\frac{dp_r}{dr} = -\kappa \frac{L(r)}{4\pi cr^2} \rho, \; p_r = \tfrac{1}{3} a T^4,\tag{5}$$

and

$$L(r) = 4\pi \int_0^r \epsilon \rho r^2 dr,\tag{6}$$

where p_r, κ, ϵ, and ρ denote, respectively, the radiation pressure, the coefficient of stellar opacity, the rate of energy generation per gram of the stellar material, and the density. Also, a is Stefan's radiation constant and c is the velocity of light.

3. The principal physical process contributing to the opacity, κ, is determined by the photo–electric absorption coefficient in the soft X–ray region, i.e., by the ionization of the innermost K- and L-shells of the highly ionized atoms.

4. With electron scattering as the ultimate source of stellar opacity, there is an upper limit to the luminosity, L, that can support a given mass M. The maximum luminosity, set by the inequality,

$$L < \frac{4\pi cGM}{\sigma_e},\tag{7}$$

where σ_e denotes the Thomson scattering-coefficient, is now generally referred to as the *Eddington limit*. This Eddington limit plays an important role in current investigations relating to X-ray sources and the luminosity of accretion discs around black holes.

5. In a first approximation, in normal stars (i.e., in stars along the main sequence) the (mass, luminosity, effective temperature)-relation is not very sensitive to the distribution of the energy sources through the star. Therefore, a relation is available for comparison with observations even in the absence of a detailed knowledge of the energy sources of the star.

6. The burning of hydrogen into helium is the most likely source of stellar energy.

No. of Globe	Radiation Pressure	Gas Pressure
30	0.00000016	0.99999984
31	0.000016	0.999984
32	0.0016	0.9984
33	0.106	0.894
34	0.570	0.430
35	0.850	0.150
36	0.951	0.049
37	0.984	0.016
38	0.9951	0.0049
39	0.9984	0.0016
40	0.99951	0.00049

These deductions, which Eddington made some sixty years ago, continue to be valid—then, as now.

I should like to expand on some of these deductions for illustrating Eddington's approach to problems of this kind.

I shall consider, first, the way Eddington established the increasing importance of radiation pressure as a factor in the equilibrium of stars of increasing mass. It will be recalled that when Eddington wrote out the mass of the sun in tons, with all the zeros explicitly, he remarked that one should not consider the exact number of zeros as of no particular consequence since "nature *does* mind."

In his *Internal Constitution of the Stars,* Eddington arrives at his conclusion by imagining a physicist

on a cloud-bound planet, who has never heard tell of the stars, calculating the ratio of radiation pressure to gas pressure for a series of globes of gas of various sizes, starting, say, with a globe of mass 10 g, then 100 g, 1000 g and so on, so that his n-th globe contains 10^n g. [Table 1] shows the more interesting part of his results.

The rest of the table would consist mainly of long strings of 9's and 0's. Just for the particular range of mass about the 33rd to 35th globes the table becomes interesting, and then lapses back into 9's and 0's again. Regarded as a tussle between matter and aether (gas pressure and radiation pressure) the contest is overwhelmingly one-sided except between numbers 33–35, where we may expect something to happen.

What "happens" is the stars.

We draw aside the veil of cloud beneath which our physicist has been working and let him look up at the sky. There he will find a thousand million globes of gas nearly all of mass between his 33rd and 35th globes—that is to say, between $\frac{1}{2}$ and 50 times the Sun's mass. The lightest known star is about $3 \cdot 10^{32}$ g and the heaviest about $2 \cdot 10^{35}$ g. The majority are between 10^{33} and 10^{34} g, where the serious challenge of radiation pressure to compete with gas pressure is beginning.[9]

The calculations of table 1 are made on the assumption that the ratio of the gas pressure (p_g) to the radiation pressure (p_r), $\beta/(1-\beta)$, is constant through the star; and that the mean molecular weight, μ, has the value 2.5. A value of $\mu = 1.0$ would have been more realistic, in which case the mass of each of the globes would have to be increased by a factor $(2.5)^2 = 6.25$. This factor is not of much consequence. But there are two important aspects of the argument on which Eddington is silent. One is that while a combination of the natural constants of the dimensions of a mass and of stellar magnitude (with all the zeros!) is clearly implied by the calculations, Eddington does not isolate it—a surprising omission in view of his later preoccupations with natural constants. Actually, the combination of natural constants which determines the masses of the globes, in the interesting range, is

$$\left[\left(\frac{k}{H}\right)^4 \frac{3}{a}\right]^{1/2} \frac{1}{G^{3/2}}, \tag{8}$$

where H is the mass of the proton, G is the constant of gravitation, and k and a are the Boltzmann and the Stefan constants, respectively. On inserting for Stefan's constant its value,

$$a = \frac{8\pi^5}{15} \frac{k^4}{h^3 c^3}, \tag{9}$$

where h is Planck's constant, we find that the combination of the natural constants, of the dimensions of a mass, that is involved is

$$\left(\frac{hc}{G}\right)^{3/2} \frac{1}{H^2} \cong 29.2 \odot \cong 5.2 \times 10^{34} \text{g}. \tag{10}$$

A case can be made that the successes of the current theories of stellar structure and stellar evolution derive in large measure from the foregoing combination of the natural constants providing a mass of the correct stellar magnitude. (I shall note in passing that the more general combination of the dimensions of a mass, namely,

$$\left(\frac{hc}{G}\right)^\alpha \frac{1}{H^{2\alpha-1}}, \tag{11}$$

where α is arbitrary, includes the Planck mass $(hc/G)^{\frac{1}{2}}$, when $\alpha = \frac{1}{2}$.)

TABLE 2

$(M/\odot)\mu^2$	Radiation Pressure	Gas Pressure
0.56	0.01	0.99
1.01	0.03	0.97
2.14	0.10	0.90
3.83	0.20	0.80
6.12	0.30	0.70
9.62	0.40	0.60
15.49	0.50	0.50
26.52	0.60	0.40
50.92	0.70	0.30
122.5	0.80	0.20
224.4	0.85	0.15
519.6	0.90	0.10

A second aspect of the calculations, presented in table 1, on which Eddington is also silent, is: Why is the extent to which radiation pressure provides support against gravity relevant to the "happening of the stars"? On this question, Eddington, instead of basing his arguments on his "standard model" (in which the ratio of the radiation pressure to the gas pressure is a constant through the star), could have used a theorem of his own—namely, that for *stability,* the pressure at the center of a star must be less than that at the center of a configuration of uniform density of the same mass and the same central density—to show that the ratio of the radiation pressure to the total pressure at the center of a star must be less than a certain fraction dependent on the mass of the star only. Table 1 would then be replaced by table 2; and the conclusion of the physicist on the cloud-bound planet would have been the same.

With regard to the other key points, the one relating to the source of stellar opacity reveals best the manner of Eddington's acceptance of physical theories when confronted with his astronomical deductions. In his considerations relating to the problem of stellar opacity, he had the benefit of consultations with C. D. Ellis who was an expert in X-ray and γ-ray physics. Also, a famous paper by H. A. Kramers provided the first theoretical evaluation of the atomic cross-sections for photo-electric ionization which Eddington needed. But prior to the publication of Kramers's paper, Eddington had developed a theory of his own based on the physically untenable hypothesis of the direct capture of electrons by atomic nuclei. And he maintained the astronomical relevance of his theory against cogent arguments by many physicists including Rutherford. And he abandoned his theory only after the appearance of Kramers's paper and the agreement of the theoretical calculations with experimental results had been demonstrated. But the comparison of astronomical observations with the theoretical mass-luminosity relation, adopting Kramers's opacity law, left a discrepancy of a factor exceeding ten. Eddington (and, independently, Strömgren) eliminated this discrepancy in 1932 by adopting the large abundances of hydrogen and helium which had, by then, been established by Russell from an analysis of the abundances of the elements in the solar atmosphere. Eddington was however slow to accept the nonuniversality of the composition of the stars that followed. Eddington had, in fact, realized much earlier that the assumption that hydrogen was abundant and that a mean molecular weight of the stars close to unity would resolve the opacity discrepancy. But this assumption would have spoiled his argument for the "happening of the stars"; and it is characteristic of Eddington that he should have concluded, "I would much prefer to find some other explanation for the discordance."

Among Eddington's predictions, that of the source of stellar energy is perhaps the most spectacular. His address, on 24 August 1920 to the British Association meeting in Cardiff, contains some of the most prescient statements in all of astronomical literature.

> Only the inertia of tradition keeps the contraction hypothesis alive—or rather, not alive, but an unburied corpse. But if we decide to inter the corpse, let us frankly recognize the position in which we are left. A star is drawing on some vast reservoir of energy by means unknown to us. This reservoir can scarcely be other than the sub-atomic energy which, it is known, exists abundantly in all matter; we sometimes dream that man will one day learn how to release it and use it for his service. The store is well-nigh inexhaustible, if only it could be tapped. There is sufficient in the Sun to maintain its output of heat for 15 billion years . . .
>
> Aston has further shown conclusively that the mass of the helium atom is even less than the sum of the masses of the four hydrogen atoms which enter into it—and in this, at any rate, the chemists agree with him. There is a loss of mass in the synthesis amounting to 1 part in 120, the atomic weight of hydrogen being 1.008 and that of helium just 4. I will not dwell on his beautiful proof of this, as you will no doubt be able to hear it from himself. Now mass cannot be annihilated, and the deficit can only represent the mass of the electrical energy set free in the transmutation. We can therefore at once calculate the quantity of energy liberated when helium is made out of hydrogen. If 5 per cent of a star's mass consists initially of hydrogen atoms, which are gradually being

combined to form more complex elements, the total heat liberated will more than suffice for our demands, and we need look no further for the source of a star's energy.

If, indeed, the sub-atomic energy in the stars is being freely used to maintain their great furnaces, it seems to bring a little nearer to fulfilment our dream of controlling this latent power for the well-being of the human race—or for its suicide.[10]

In this context of the source of stellar energy, astrophysicists of an earlier generation will recall Eddington's famous retort:

It has, for example, been objected that the temperature of the stars is not great enough for the transmutation of hydrogen into helium—so ruling out one possible source of energy. But helium exists, and it is not much use for the critic to urge that the stars are not hot enough for its formation unless he is prepared to show us a hotter place.[11]

V

I stated at the outset that Eddington's interest in the internal constitution of the stars arose from his efforts to find an explanation for stellar variability and the period-luminosity relation exhibited by the Cepheids. Eddington first generalized Ritter's earlier analysis of the adiabatic pulsations of gaseous stars in convective equilibrium to the case of a star in radiative equilibrium built on his standard model. Then combining the resulting formula for the period with his mass-luminosity relation, Eddington was able to account, in a general way, for the observed period-luminosity relation of the Cepheids. The pulsation theory of stellar variability thus came to be established.

Eddington's preliminary analysis of Cepheid variability did not provide the correct phase relationships among the various variables such as the brightness, the effective temperature, and the radial velocity of the star. However, he clearly realized that these phase relationships can be understood only by a careful examination of the mechanism of energy transfer in the outer layers of the star where the abundant elements, hydrogen and helium, get ionized and zones of convection are formed. He returned to this problem several times in later years. Indeed, one of his last published papers is devoted to this problem. But the final solution was found only later by the combined investigations of M. Schwarzschild, P. Ledoux, and R. Christy.

While Eddington's major contributions to astrophysics lay in the domain of stellar structure, his contributions to other areas of astrophysics are by no means insignificant. He devised a method of approximation—the "Eddington approximation"—for solving problems in radiative transfer. His solution for the problem of line formation in stellar atmospheres, for example, was much in use during the pioneering years in the theory of stellar atmospheres. He also considered the effect of reflexion in close binaries—an effect which one must allow for in analyzing the light curves of eclipsing binaries for the determination of the masses of the components. The problem Eddington considered in this latter context is the prototype of the larger problem of the diffuse reflexion and transmission of light by plane-parallel atmospheres—a subject which grew to maturity in later years.

In these other areas of astrophysics, perhaps the most important is Eddington's introduction of a *"dilution factor"*—a word he coined and still in current usage—to allow for the reduced intensity of the prevailing radiation-field in determining the state of ionization in interstellar space. Eddington was also the first to adapt to the problem of *interstellar* absorption-lines the method of the "curve of growth" which A. Unsold and M. Minnaert had developed for determining the relative abundances of the elements from the intensities of *stellar* absorption-lines.

Eddington's interests in galactic dynamics and astrophysics converged in his prediction that the radial velocities, determined from interstellar absorption-lines, must show, in their dependence on galactic latitude, an amplitude which is one-half of that shown by the stellar absorption-lines. This prediction was later beautifully confirmed by the observations of O. Struve and J. S. Plaskett.

Of the *Internal Constitution of the Stars,* which includes most of what I have described so far, Russell has said, "This volume has every claim to be regarded as a masterpiece of the first rank."[12]

VI

In my account of Eddington's contributions to the constitution of the stars, I did not make any reference to the running controversies he had, first with Jeans and later with Milne. From the vantage point of the present, the questions that were at issue then do not seem to be very relevant: with the understanding of the source of stellar energy, the unresolved issues have required different formulations and different solutions. It should, however, be stated that Eddington was not always fair in the way he treated his scientific adversaries. For example, after a paper by Milne presented at the December 1929 meeting of the Royal Astronomical Society, Eddington's response, in part, was:

> Prof. Milne did not enter into detail as to why he arrives at results so widely different from my own; and my interest in the rest of the paper

is dimmed because it would be absurd to pretend that I think there is the remotest chance of his being right.[13]

And the acrimony with which the discussions were sometimes carried out is sufficiently illustrated by the following extracts from two letters of Jeans published in the *Observatory:*

> So much work has been done on isothermal equilibrium that it is difficult to understand how Prof. Eddington can harbour the illusion that he is doing pioneer work in unexplored territory, yet his complete absence of reference to other theoretical workers (except for some numerical computations quoted from Emden) suggests that such is actually the case. (August 1926)

> May I conclude by assuring Prof. Eddington it would give me great pleasure if he could remove a long-standing source of friction between us by abstaining in future from making wild attacks on my work which he cannot substantiate, and by making the usual acknowledgements whenever he finds that my previous work is of use to him? I attach all the more importance to the second part of the request, because I find that some of the most fruitful ideas which I have introduced into astronomical physics—e.g., the annihilation of matter as a source of stellar energy, and highly dissociated atoms and free electrons as the substance of the stars—are by now fairly generally attributed to Prof. Eddington. (November 1926)[14]

I should like to leave these unhappy episodes with an anecdote in a lighter vein.

It is known that Eddington, on occasions, enjoyed seeing horse races and that, not infrequently, took his sister to the Newmarket races. G. H. Hardy must have known of this, for I heard him once ask Eddington if he had ever bet on a horse. Eddington admitted that he had, "but just once." Hardy was curious to know the occasion; and Eddington explained that a horse named Jeans was running and that he could not resist the temptation of betting on it. Questioned whether he had won, Eddington responded with his characteristic smile and a "No!"

* * *

Eddington: The expositor and the exponent of general relativity

My last lecture was devoted mostly to Eddington's contributions to theoretical astrophysics and to justifying Russell's assessment of him as the most distinguished representative of astrophysics of his time. In this lecture, I shall turn to Eddington as an expositor and an exponent of the general theory of relativity, to the part he played in the Greenwich-Cambridge expeditions to observe the solar eclipse of 29 May 1919 with the express purpose of verifying Einstein's prediction of the deflection of light by a gravitational field, and to his efforts, extending over sixteen years, in cosmology and—quoting his own description—in "unifying quantum theory and relativity theory." But in contrast to my last lecture, I am afraid that this lecture will not altogether be a happy one.

I shall begin with the happier side.

VII

After founding the principles of the special theory of relativity in 1905, Einstein's principal preoccupation in the following ten years was to bring the Newtonian theory of gravitation into conformity with those same principles and, in particular, with the requirement that no signal be propagated with a velocity exceeding that of light. After many false starts, Einstein achieved his goal in a spectacular series of short communications to the Berlin Academy of Sciences during the summer and autumn of 1915. Because of the war, the news of Einstein's success would not have crossed the English Channel (not to mention the Atlantic Ocean) had it not been for the neutrality of the Netherlands and Einstein's personal friendship with Lorentz, Ehrenfest, and deSitter (see fig. 3). DeSitter sent copies of Einstein's papers to Eddington, and he further communicated to the Royal Astronomical Society, during 1916–17, three papers of his own in part expository and in part original contributions. What has now come to be called deSitter's universe is described in the last of the three papers.

Eddington, as the Secretary of the Royal Astronomical Society at that time, had to deal with deSitter's papers. One may presume, from his account of the last of the three papers at the December 1917 meeting of the Royal Astronomical Society, that he had read the papers carefully and refereed them himself.[15]

FIG. 3 (*clockwise from upper left*) A. Einstein, P. Ehrenfest, W. deSitter, H. A. Lorentz, A. S. Eddington.

This photograph is a reproduction of one presented to the author by J. H. Oort (formerly Director of the Leiden Observatory, Holland) in 1953 with the note that it "was taken by deSitter's oldest son (now professor of geology in Leiden) on 26 September 1923. The picture was taken in deSitter's study . . . We recently found the original negative."

It will be recalled that in the last of the communications in which Einstein formulated his fundamental field equations, he concluded with the prophetic statement, "anyone who fully comprehends this theory cannot escape its magic." Eddington must surely have been caught in its magic; for, within two years, he had written his *Report on the Relativity Theory of Gravitation* for the Physical Society of London, a report that must have been written in white heat. Eddington's *Report* is written so clearly and yet so concisely that it can be read, even today, as a good introductory text by a beginning student.

VIII

Eddington's enthusiasm for the general theory of relativity must have succeeded in ensnaring into its magic his close friend and associate Sir Frank Dyson, the Astronomer Royal; for together, they were soon planning expeditions to observe the solar eclipse of 29 May 1919 if, to quote Jeans, "the state of civilization should permit when the time came." Eddington has described his own part in the planning and in the successful outcome of the expeditions "as the most exciting event, I recall, in my connection with astronomy." The story has so many interesting facets that it is hard to know where to begin. I hope you will forgive me if I begin with an account which Eddington gave me.

I once expressed to Eddington my admiration of his scientific sensibility in planning the expeditions under circumstances when the future must have appeared very bleak. To my surprise, Eddington disclaimed any credit on that account and told me that, had he been left to himself, he would not have planned the expeditions since he was fully convinced of the truth of the general theory of relativity! And he told me how his part in the expeditions came about. I have written about it in the *Notes and Records of the Royal Society*[16]; but perhaps you will allow me to repeat it.

In 1917, after more than two years of war, England enacted conscription for all able-bodied men; and Eddington, who was then thirty-four, was eligible for draft. But as a practising and devout Quaker, he was a conscientious objector; and it was known and expected that he would claim deferment from military service on that account. Now the climate of opinion in England during World War I was very adverse with respect to conscientious objectors: it was in fact a social disgrace to be associated with one. And the stalwarts of the Cambridge of those days, Sir Joseph Larmor (of the Larmor precession), Professor H. F. Newall, and others tried through the Home Office to have Eddington deferred on the grounds that he was a most distinguished scientist and that it was not in Britain's long-range interests to have Eddington serve in the army. The case of Moseley, killed in action at Gallipoli, was very much in the minds of British scientists. And Larmor and others very nearly succeeded in their efforts. A letter from the Home Office was sent to Eddington, and all he had to do was to sign his name and return it. But Eddington added a postscript to the effect that if he were not deferred on the stated ground, he would claim it on grounds of conscientious objection anyway. This postscript naturally placed the Home Office in a logical quandary since a confessed conscientious objector must be sent to a camp; and Larmor and others were very much piqued. But as Eddington told me, he could see no reason for their pique. As he expressed himself, many of his Quaker friends found themselves in camps in Northern England peeling potatoes, and he saw no reason why he should not join them. In any event, apparently at Dyson's intervention—as the Astronomer Royal he had close connections with the Admiralty—Eddington was deferred with the express stipulation that if the war should end by May 1919, then Eddington should undertake to lead an expedition for the purpose of verifying Einstein's prediction!

Slightly different accounts of these incidents have been published; but they differ only in the emphasis and in the overtones. In any event, we are fortunate in having an account of the planning and the execution of the expeditions by Eddington himself. He writes:

> The bending affects stars seen near the sun, and accordingly the only chance of making the observation is during a total eclipse when the moon cuts off the dazzling light. Even then there is a great deal of light from the sun's corona which stretches far above the disc. It is thus necessary to have rather bright stars near the sun, which will not be lost in the glare of the corona. Further, the displacements of these stars can only be measured relatively to other stars, preferably more distant from the sun and less displaced; we need therefore a reasonable number of outer bright stars to serve as reference points.
>
> In a superstitious age a natural philosopher wishing to perform an important experiment would consult an astrologer to ascertain an auspicious moment for the trial. With better reason, an astronomer today consulting the stars would announce that the most favourable day of the year for weighing light is May 29. The reason is that the sun in its annual journey round the ecliptic goes through fields of stars of varying richness, but on May 29 it is in the midst of a quite exceptional patch of bright stars—part of Hyades—by far the best star-field encountered. Now if this problem had been put forward at some other period of history, it might have been necessary to wait some thousands of years

for a total eclipse of the sun to happen on the lucky date. But by strange good fortune an eclipse did happen on May 29, 1919 . . .

Attention was called to this remarkable opportunity by the Astronomer Royal (Sir Frank Dyson) in March 1917; and preparations were begun by a committee of the Royal Society and Royal Astronomical Society for making the observations . . . [17]

. . . Plans were begun in 1918 during the war, and it was doubtful until the eleventh hour whether there would be any possibility of the expeditions starting . . . Two expeditions were organized at Greenwich by Sir Frank Dyson, the one going to Sobral in Brazil and the other to the Isle of Principe in West Africa. Dr. A. C. D. Crommelin and Mr. C. Davidson went to Sobral; and Mr. E. T. Cottingham and the writer went to Principe.

It was impossible to get any work done by instrument-makers until after the armistice; and, as the expeditions had to sail in February, there was a tremendous rush of preparation. The Brazil party had perfect weather for the eclipse; through incidental circumstances, their observations could not be reduced until some months later, but in the end they provided the most conclusive confirmation. I was at Principe. There the eclipse day came with rain and cloud-covered sky, which almost took away all hope. Near totality the sun began to show dimly; and we carried through the programme hoping that the conditions might not be so bad as they seemed. The cloud must have thinned before the end of totality, because amid many failures we obtained two plates showing the desired star-images. These were compared with plates already taken of the same star-field at a time when the sun was elsewhere, so that the difference indicated the apparent displacement of the stars due to the bending of the light-rays in passing near the sun.

As the problem then presented itself to us, there were three possibilities. There might be no deflection at all; that is to say, light might not be subject to gravitation. There might be a "half-deflection," signifying that light was subject to gravitation, as Newton had suggested, and obeyed the simple Newtonian law. Or there might be a "full-deflection," confirming Einstein's instead of Newton's law. I remember Dyson explaining all this to my companion Cottingham, who gathered the main idea that the bigger the result, the more exciting it would be. "What will it mean if we get double the deflection?" "Then," said Dyson, "Eddington will go mad, and you will have to come home alone."

Arrangements had been made to measure the plates on the spot, not entirely from impatience, but as a precaution against mishap on the way home, so one of the successful plates was examined immediately. The quantity to be looked for was large as astronomical measures go, so that one plate would virtually decide the question, though, of course, confirmation from others would be sought. Three days after the eclipse, as the last lines of the calculations were reached, I knew that Einstein's theory had stood the test and the new outlook of scientific thought must prevail. Cottingham did not have to go home alone.[18]

The scientific results of the expedition were reported at a joint meeting of the Royal Society and the Royal Astronomical Society on 6 November 1919 with Sir J. J. Thomson, President of the Royal Society, in the Chair. This meeting was surrounded by an unusual amount of publicity; the extent of it was recalled by Rutherford on an occasion that I well remember.

It was during the Christmas recess of 1933 when, after dinner in Hall at Trinity, Rutherford, Eddington, Patrick DuVal (a distinguished geometer), Sir Maurice Amos (at one time, during the 1920s, the Chief Judicial Advisor to the Egyptian Government), and I sat around the fire in the Senior Combination Room, in conversation. At some point during the conversation, Sir Maurice Amos turned to Rutherford and said, "I do not see why Einstein is accorded a greater public acclaim than you. After all, you invented the nuclear model of the atom; and that model provides the basis for all of physical science today and it is even more universal in its applications than Newton's laws of gravitation. Also, Einstein's predictions refer to such minute departures from the Newtonian theory that I do not see what all the fuss is about." Rutherford, in response, turned to Eddington and said, "You are responsible for Einstein's fame." And, more seriously, he continued:

> The war had just ended; and the complacency of the Victorian and the Edwardian times had been shattered. The people felt that all their values and all their ideals had lost their bearings. Now, suddenly, they learnt that an astronomical prediction by a German scientist had been confirmed by expeditions to Brazil and West Africa and, indeed, prepared for already during the war, by British astronomers. Astronomy had always appealed to public imagination; and an astronomical discovery, transcending worldly strife, struck a responsive chord. The meeting of the Royal Society, at which the results of the British expeditions were reported, was headlined in all the British papers: and the typhoon of publicity crossed the Atlantic. From that point on, the American press played Einstein to the maximum.

I will conclude this account by quoting Jeans when he presented the Gold Medal of the Royal Astronomical Society to Dyson:

In 1918, in the darkest days of the war, two expeditions were planned, one by Greenwich Observatory and one by Cambridge, to observe, if the state of civilization should permit when the time came, the eclipse of May 1919, with a view to a crucial test of Einstein's generalized relativity. The armistice was signed in November 1918; the expeditions went, and returned bringing back news which changed, and that irrevocably, the astronomer's conception of the nature of gravitation and the ordinary man's conception of the nature of the universe in which he lives. If the credit of this achievement had to be divided between Sir Frank Dyson and Professor Eddington I frankly do not know in what proportion the division should be made. To my mind, however, it is not so much an occasion for sharing out credit as for attributing the whole credit to each, for if either had failed to play his part, either from want of vision, of enthusiasm, or of capacity of seizing the right moment, I doubt if the expeditions would have gone at all, and the great credit of first determining observationally what sort of things space and time really are would probably have gone elsewhere.[19]

IX

I should like to add a few footnotes to the story.

At the conclusion of the reports by Dyson and by Eddington on the results of their expeditions, J. J. Thomson made the following remarks from the Chair:

> Newton did, in fact, suggest this very point in the first query in his "Optics," and his suggestion would presumably have led to the half-value. But this result is not an isolated one; it is part of a whole continent of scientific ideas affecting the most fundamental concepts of physics . . . This is the most important result obtained in connection with the theory of gravitation since Newton's day, and it is fitting that it should be announced at a meeting of the *Society* so closely connected with him . . .
>
> If his theory is right, it makes us take an entirely new view of gravitation. If it is sustained that Einstein's reasoning holds good—and it has survived two very severe tests in connection with the perihelion of Mercury and the present eclipse—then it is the result of one of the highest achievements of human thought. The weak point in the theory is the great difficulty in expressing it. It would seem that no one can understand the new law of gravitation without a thorough knowledge of the theory of invariants and of the calculus of variations.[20]

The "difficulty" of understanding the general theory of relativity, to which J. J. Thomson referred, was then, and for a long time, a prevalent view. Indeed, a myth soon arose that "only three persons in the world understood general relativity." The myth, in fact, had its origin at this same meeting.

Eddington recalled (during the after-dinner conversation at Trinity to which I referred earlier) that, as the joint meeting of the Royal Society and the Royal Astronomical Society was dispersing, Ludwig Silberstein came up to him and said, "Professor Eddington, you must be one of three persons in the world who understands general relativity." On Eddington's demurring to this statement, Silberstein responded, "Don't be modest, Eddington," and Eddington replied that, "On the contrary, I am trying to think who the third person is."

I may parenthetically remark that this supposed difficulty in understanding the general theory of relativity was greatly exaggerated: it contributed to the stagnation of the subject for several decades. Many of the developments of the sixties and the seventies could easily have taken place during the twenties and the thirties.

Eddington was very fond of repeating Dyson's remark to Cottingham, "Eddington will go mad, and you will have to come home alone." Thus when, at a meeting of the Royal Astronomical Society in January 1932, Finlay Freundlich reported that the results of *his* eclipse expedition gave for the deflection of light a value substantially in excess of Einstein's prediction,[21] Eddington repeated Dyson's remark with devastating effect! But when the concordant results of the Lick Observatory expedition of 1922 were reported at the April 1923 meeting of the Royal Astronomical Society, Eddington's comment was:

> I think that it was Bellman in "The Hunting of the Snark" who laid down the rule, "When I say it three times, it is right." The stars have now said it three times to three separate expeditions; and I am convinced their answer is right.[22]

And finally, I want to refer to a problem in probability theory which attained some notoriety in the late thirties and which had its origin in the Greenwich-Cambridge expeditions. The problem and the manner of its solution by Eddington reveal his insight into probability theory—a theory in which (as in *Combination of Observations*) he had become interested when he had to combine a large body of uncertain observations in his investigations in star streaming.

You will recall that the two eclipse expeditions were in charge, respectively, of Crommelin and Davidson (who went to Sobral) and of Eddington and Cottingham (who went to Príncipe). In an after-dinner speech, before the expeditions departed, Crommelin hinted that the following situation might arise:

If C, C', D, and E each speak the truth once in three times, independently, and C affirms that C' denies that D declares that E is a liar, what is the probability that E was speaking the truth?

Eddington stated this problem with A, B, C, and D substituted for C, C', D, and E in his *New Pathways in Science*[23] and gave the solution as 25/71. He later stated that "when I rashly gave my solution, I did not foresee a considerable increase in my correspondence." Many, including Dingle, argued that the problem, as formulated, was ambiguous and that Eddington's solution was not, by any means, the most obvious one. Eddington meant the problem to assert (as anyone unsophisticated will agree) that two statements had been made:[24]

(1) D made a statement, say, X;

and

(2) A made the statement that "B denies that C contradicted X."

What is required is the probability that X is true. Eddington explained his solution as follows:

> We do not know that B and C made any relevant statements. For example, if B truthfully denied that C contradicted X, there is no reason to suppose that C affirmed X.
>
> It will be found that the only combinations inconsistent with the data are:
> (α) A truths, B lies, C truths, D truths;
> (β) A truths, B lies, C lies, D lies.
> For if A is lying, we do not know what B said; and if A and B both truthed, we do not know what C said.
>
> Since (α) and (β) occur respectively twice and eight times out of 81 occasions, D's 27 truths and 54 lies are reduced to 25 truths and 46 lies. The probability is therefore 25/71.[25]

Eddington's solution is certainly correct, though dissents continue to be expressed.

X

I now turn to other facets of Eddington's contributions to classical relativity. It is my judgment that Eddington's greatest contribution to the general theory of relativity is his wondrous treatment of the subject in his *Mathematical Theory of Relativity*. I continue to use it. Besides, the mathematical treatment is interspersed with many striking aphorisms. The one I like best is: "Space is not a lot of points close together; it is a lot of distances interlocked."[26]

The following extracts from a review of the book by his "adversary," Jeans, summarizes very well its distinguishing features:

> Everywhere we find indications of ungrudged labour and scrupulous care; we read section after section and each time feel that the matter could not have been better put. Owing to the care which has been expended upon it, the mathematician will read the book with ease and pleasure . . .
> The style of the book is admirably clear and concise throughout; we can give it no higher praise than to say that it is fully up to the high standard which Prof. Eddington has led us to expect from him.[27]

Departing from generalities, I should like to dwell briefly on three specific investigations which illustrate Eddington's perception and understanding of classical relativity.

First, most modern students of relativity will be familiar with the fact that the apparent singularity of the Schwarzschild metric at what is now designated as the event horizon is a consequence of the chosen coordinate system and has no further significance. In 1924, Eddington explicitly gave a transformation—now called the Eddington-Finkelstein transformation—which makes this fact manifest.[28] It should, however, be stated that Eddington obtained his transformation for a different purpose and it is not clear from the context that he was addressing himself to the problem of the coordinate singularity.

Second, in view of the current arguments over the validity or otherwise of Einstein's original formula for the rate of emission of gravitational radiation in terms of the varying quadrupole moment of the source, it is interesting to recall that Eddington made, as early as 1922, an explicit *ab initio* calculation of the rate of emission of gravitational energy by a rigid spinning rod and obtained the correct answer, discovering incidentally a numerical error of a factor 2 in Einstein's original formula.[29]

Third, in an investigation published in 1938, Eddington and Clark, independently of Einstein, Infeld, and Hoffmann, considered the *n*-body problem in general relativity and solved for the metric coefficients in what we should now call the first post-Newtonian approximation.[30] Eddington and Clark did not, however, reduce the problem to the Hamiltonian form nor did they obtain the analogues of the classical ten integrals of the equations of motion. They were primarily concerned with the motion of the center of mass. The general solution to their problem requires one to obtain the coordinate transformation, consistently in the first post-Newtonian approximation, between any two frames of reference in uniform relative motion, i.e., a *post-Galilean transformation*. Eddington and Clark did not obtain such a transformation; but they did solve a restricted problem in the relative motion of two mass-points to which they had addressed themselves.

The foregoing examples, particularly the last one, show that Eddington, if he cared, could formulate and solve problems of depth and complexity in the classical theory of relativity. But he does not seem to have cared much.

XI

Of his contributions to classical relativity, Eddington attached the greatest importance to his generalization of Weyl's theory attempting to unify gravitation and electromagnetism. Indeed, in a document[31] discovered among his papers in 1954, Eddington, in an impersonal statement of what he considered as his major scientific accomplishments, gives a prominent place to his generalization of Weyl's theory and "connected with this, his explanation of the law of gravitation," $G_{\mu\nu} = \Lambda g_{\mu\nu}$, where Λ is the cosmical constant. In any event, the attitude of mind that he formed, in this context at this time, was to crystallize in later years to become a permanent bedrock. For this reason, I shall try to explain briefly the nature of Weyl's theory and Eddington's generalization of it.

At the time Einstein formulated his general theory of relativity, it was thought that the entire physical world required for its description only two fields: the gravitational field and the electromagnetic field. Since Einstein had shown how the gravitational field can be absorbed into the structure of space-time, it was natural that efforts should have been made to absorb the electromagnetic field into the structure of space-time, as well. Clearly, if one is to achieve such a synthesis, one must enlarge the geometrical base of Einstein's theory by a suitable generalization of Riemannian geometry. Weyl and Eddington sought such a generalization in the net effect of displacing a vector, parallel to itself, around a closed infinitesimal contour. In Riemannian geometry, a vector, after describing such a closed contour, is altered in its direction, but is unchanged in its length. Weyl supposed that the length is also changed by an amount proportional to its initial length; and Eddington allowed the change in length to be arbitrary (in the first instance).

In Weyl's theory, consistently with its underlying assumptions, the Christoffel connection, $\Gamma_{ij,k}$ of Riemannian geometry is replaced by

(12) $$\Gamma^*_{ij,k} = \Gamma_{ij,k} + \tfrac{1}{2}(g_{ik}\phi_j + g_{jk}\phi_i - g_{ij}\phi_k),$$

where ϕ_i, $i = 1, 2, 3, 4$, are some smooth functions. Also, in Weyl's theory, we should require that all geometrical relations and physical laws are invariant not only to arbitrary coordinate transformations (as in Einstein's theory) but also to *gauge transformations,* i.e., to the substitution

$$\phi_i \rightarrow \phi_i - \frac{1}{\lambda} \frac{\partial \lambda}{\partial x^i}, \qquad (13)$$

where λ is an arbitrary function. With these postulates, Weyl showed that

$$F_{ik} = \frac{\partial \phi_k}{\partial x^i} - \frac{\partial \phi_i}{\partial x^k}, \qquad (14)$$

has all the properties of the Maxwell tensor; and he achieved the unification of gravitation and electromagnetism in this fashion.

The most important consequence of Weyl's theory, for the theory of gravitation, is that in the absence of an electromagnetic field, Einstein's equation (for the vacuum),

$$G_{ij} = 0, \qquad (15)$$

is replaced by

$$G_{ij} = \Lambda g_{ij}, \qquad (16)$$

where Λ is a universal constant, and g_{ij} and G_{ij} are, respectively, the metric tensor and the Einstein tensor. The constant Λ in equation (16) is the *cosmical constant* which Einstein had introduced earlier in 1917, as an afterthought, in order that his theory may allow a static, homogeneous, and isotropic model for the universe.

Eddington's generalization of Weyl's theory amounts to replacing equation (12) by

$$\Gamma^*_{ij,k} = \Gamma_{ij,k} + K_{ik,j} + K_{jk,i} - K_{ij,k}, \qquad (17)$$

where $K_{ik,j}$ is some covariant tensor of rank 3 (unspecified at this stage). And again, in the absence of an electromagnetic field, we are led to Einstein's equation including the term in the cosmical constant.

The fact that, by the foregoing equations, we are naturally led to the term in the cosmical constant, convinced Eddington of the *necessity* of including it in Einstein's equation; and it became central to his views. As he explained it:

> The radius of curvature at any point and in any direction is in constant proportion to the length of a specified material unit placed at the same point and oriented in the same direction.[32]

Or, conversely,

> The length of a specified material structure bears a constant ratio to the radius of curvature of the world at the place and in the direction in which it lies.

Eddington states this central doctrine of his in a variety of ways. Thus,

> We see that Einstein's law of gravitation is the almost inevitable outcome of the use of material-measuring appliances for surveying the world, whatever may be the actual laws under which material structures are adjusted in equilibrium with the empty space around them.[33]

Or, again,

> An electron would not know how large it ought to be unless there existed independent lengths in space for it to measure itself against.[34]

Indeed, Eddington considered that reverting to Einstein's equation without the Λ-term is tantamount to reverting to Newtonian theory:

> I would as soon think of reverting to Newtonian theory as of dropping the cosmical constant.[35]

This absolute conviction of his resulted in such extreme statements as the following:

> To set $\Lambda = 0$, implies a reversion to the imperfectly relativistic theory—a step which is no more to be thought of than of a return to the Newtonian theory.[36]
> . . . The position of the cosmical constant seems to me impregnable; and if ever the theory of relativity falls into disrepute the cosmical constant will be the last stronghold to collapse. To drop the cosmical constant would knock the bottom out of space.[37]

Eddington, however, was not alone in his views. I once asked Lemaître, sometime during the late fifties, what, in his judgment, was the most important change wrought by the general theory of relativity in our basic physical concepts. His answer, without a moment's hesitation, was "the introduction of the cosmical constant!" Similarly, in a letter to Niels Bohr in 1923, Einstein states, unequivocally, "Eddington has come closer to the truth than Weyl."[38] Indeed, one of the last "unified field-theories" which Einstein (and, independently, Schrodinger) developed has much in common with Eddington's generalization of Weyl's theory. But Weyl's views were different. He wrote in 1953:

As to Eddington's own creative contributions to the theory, I would say that they consist chiefly of two things: first his idea of an affine field theory, and then his later attempts to explain by epistemological reasons the pure numbers that seem to enter into the constitution of the universe . . .

His first contribution certainly has borne fruit. Einstein himself took it up when he formulated an action principle for such a theory (which Eddington, I believe erroneously, had thought unnecessary) . . .

. . . but I am quite sceptical also about Einstein's most recent unitary field theory. I am pretty sure that the last word on the nature of gravitation is not yet spoken, and I am inclined to believe that it lies in a direction quite different from Eddington's and Einstein's last ideas. The riddle may have to wait a long time for its solution.[39]

In spite of Eddington's positive views, the subsequent history of the cosmical constant has been a checkered one. When Friedmann's cosmological models were found to provide an adequate base for accounting for the simple fact of the Hubble expansion, Einstein and deSitter, in a joint paper, stated that one can do without the cosmical constant. In view of the many exaggerated statements that have been made concerning this supposed "retraction" of Λ, it is of interest to record precisely what it was they said.

Historically the term containing the "cosmological constant" Λ was introduced into the field equations in order to enable us to account theoretically for the existence of a finite mean density in a static universe. It now appears that in the dynamical case this end can be reached without the introduction of Λ . . .

. . . The curvature [constant Λ] is, however, essentially determinable, and an increase in the precision of data derived from observations will enable us in the future to fix its sign and to determine its value.[40]

Eddington has written of his meeting with Einstein and of a communication from deSitter, soon after the publication of their paper, which throws an interesting sidelight on this matter (and doubt on the extreme statements that have been attributed to Einstein with respect to his retraction):

Einstein came to stay with me shortly afterwards, and I took him to task about it. He replied: "I did not think the paper very important myself, but deSitter was keen on it." Just after Einstein had gone, deSitter wrote to me announcing a visit. He added: "You will have seen the paper by Einstein and myself. I do not myself consider the result of much importance, but Einstein seemed to think that it was."[41]

What is the present view, then, on the cosmical constant? One can discern the prevalence of two views: an *extreme view* (expressed, for example, by W. Pauli[42]) that the cosmological term "is superfluous, not justified, and should be rejected"; and a *moderate view* (expressed, for example, by W. Rindler[43]) that the cosmological term "belongs to the field equations, much as an additive constant belongs to an indefinite integral." There is much to recommend the moderate view, since the term in Λ is of no consequence except in the cosmological context, and its inclusion hardly increases the complexity of the solutions for the cosmological models one generally considers. In any event, it is clear that no serious student of relativity is likely to subscribe to Eddington's view that "to set $\Lambda = 0$ is to knock the bottom out of space."

XII

Let me conclude this part of my consideration of Eddington's work with an anecdote in a lighter vein.

Eddington visited the Physics Department of the University of California at Berkeley in 1924. On that occasion, he shared an office with one Professor W. H. Williams with whom he played golf twice a week at the Claremont Club. On the eve of his departure, the Faculty Club arranged a dinner in Eddington's honor; and Professor Williams was asked to give a speech. As Professor Williams wrote,[44]

. . . after some efforts towards solemnity, I descended to doggerel. Eddington, as you know, was an *Alice in Wonderland* fan. This and the allied topsy-turvydom of Carroll and Einstein, together with the irreverent way we both treated the royal game of golf, furnished the motive for the following poem.

THE EINSTEIN AND THE EDDINGTON

The sun was setting on the links,
    The moon looked down serene,
The caddies all had gone to bed,
    But still there could be seen
Two players lingering by the trap
    That guards the thirteenth green.

The Einstein and the Eddington
    Were counting up their score;
The Einstein's card showed ninety-eight
    And Eddington's was more.
And both lay bunkered in the trap
    And both stood there and swore.

I hate to see, the Einstein said;
    Such quantities of sand;
Just why they placed a bunker here
    I cannot understand.
If one could smooth this landscape out,
    I think it would be grand.

If seven maids with seven mops
    Would sweep the fairway clean
I'm sure that I could make this hole
    In less than seventeen.
I doubt it, said the Eddington,
    Your slice is pretty mean.

Then all the little golf balls came
    To see what they were at,
And some of them were tall and thin
    And some were short and fat,
A few of them were round and smooth,
    But most of them were flat.

The time has come, said Eddington,
    To talk of many things:
Of cubes and clocks and meter-sticks
    And why a pendulum swings.
And how far space is out of plumb,
    And whether time has wings.

I learned at school the apple's fall
    To gravity was due.
But now you tell me that the cause
    Is merely $G_{\mu\nu}$,
I cannot bring myself to think
    That this is really true.

You say that gravitation's force
    Is clearly not a pull.
That space is mostly emptiness,
    While time is nearly full;
And though I hate to doubt your word,
    It sounds a bit like bull.

And space, it has dimensions four,
    Instead of only three.
The square on the hypotenuse
    Ain't what it used to be.

It grieves me sore, the things you've done
    To plane geometry.

You hold that time is badly warped,
    That even light is bent:
I think I get the idea there,
    If this is what you meant:
The mail the postman brings today,
    Tomorrow will be sent.

If I should go to Timbuctoo
    With twice the speed of light,
And leave this afternoon at four,
    I'd get back home last night.
You've got it now, the Einstein said,
    That is precisely right.

But if the planet Mercury
    In going round the sun,
Never returns to where it was
    Until its course is run,
The things we started out to do
    Were better not begun.

And if, before the past is through,
    The future intervenes;
Then what's the use of anything;
    Of cabbages or queens?
Pray tell me what's the bally use
    Of Presidents and Deans.

The shortest line, Einstein replied,
    Is not the one that's straight;
It curves around upon itself,
    Much like a figure eight,
And if you go too rapidly
    You will arrive too late.

But Easter day is Christmas time
    And far away is near,
And two and two is more than four
    And over there is here.
You may be right, said Eddington,
    It seems a trifle queer.

But thank you very, very much,
    For troubling to explain;
I hope you will forgive my tears,
    My head begins to pain;
I feel the symptoms coming on
    Of softening of the brain.

XIII

My discussion, so far, has been concerned, principally, with Eddington's contributions to astrophysics and to classical relativity up to the
middle twenties. In 1926, when his *Internal Constitution of the Stars* was
published, Eddington was forty-four years old. For the following
eighteen years, except for occasional excursions into areas of his earlier
interests, Eddington was preoccupied with justifying a particular cosmological model of his choice, a model which he further made the
basis for his "fundamental theory unifying quantum theory and relativity theory." I do not make claims to understand, in any real sense,
Eddington's fundamental theory. But there are two premises which,
by Eddington's own statements, are basic to his theory. And these two
premises, to the extent I can judge, are either not valid or not accepted.
But first, I should explain, as objectively as I can, Eddington's perception of the cosmological aspects of the problem.

At the time Eddington wrote his *Mathematical Theory of Relativity*
there were two models of the universe[45] both dependent on a nonvanishing cosmical constant Λ: Einstein's universe which is static and in
hydro-static equilibrium and deSitter's universe which is also static but
expanding. Both models are theoretically possible and consistent with
the assumptions of homogeneity and isotropy. Since in deSitter's universe there is an expansion, with distant objects receding with increasing velocity, while in Einstein's universe there is no such expansion,
Eddington, already in his *Mathematical Theory of Relativity,* expresses
himself more favorably to deSitter's universe as a model for the astronomical universe, on the strength of some very meagre observational
data that were available to him at that time.

Both Einstein's and deSitter's universes are static in the sense that
none of the metric coefficients are dependent on time. It was realized
later that the static character of deSitter's universe, in spite of the expansion which it exhibits, is derived from the absence of any mass-
density in it. Therefore, Einstein's universe was, at that time, the only
model of the universe which had no motions in it. As Eddington
summed up the situation:

> Einstein's universe contains matter but no motion; deSitter's universe contains motion but no matter.[46]

However, in a paper published in 1922, A. Friedmann had shown that Einstein's equation allowed nonstatic models for the universe which are homogeneous and isotropic. Independently of Friedmann, Lemaître rediscovered the same solutions in 1927 and developed in some detail the astronomical consequences of the theory. Eddington came to know of Lemaître's paper and gave it wide publicity in his writings. Since Λ now became a parameter to which one may assign positive, zero, or negative values, one had a range of cosmological models to choose from. These models continue to provide the basis for comparisons with astronomical observations. But from the outset, Eddington's interests were focused on a particular member of the sequence of possible models. The model he preferred was one in which the universe was initially an Einstein universe with its mass (M) and Radius (R_E) related in the manner

$$(18) \qquad \Lambda = \frac{1}{R_E} \text{ and } \frac{GM}{c^2} = \tfrac{1}{2}\pi R_E;$$

and later by virtue of its instability (a fact which had been demonstrated by Lemaître), the universe began expanding. It could have contracted just as well; but Eddington and others showed that an initial condensation is more likely to lead to an expansion than to a contraction.

Why did Eddington choose this particular model for the description of the astronomical universe? As he explained:

> I am a detective in search of a criminal—the cosmical constant. I know he exists, but I do not know his appearance; for instance I do not know if he is a little man or a tall man.[47]

And the way Eddington endeavored to find the "appearance" of his "criminal" is roughly along the following lines.

In Dirac's equation for an electron, moving in the electromagnetic field of a fixed electric charge, the term which involves its mass, m_e, is $m_e c^2/e^2$. Eddington argued that this term arises by virtue of the existence of all the other particles in the universe. More precisely, he considered it as a consequence of the "energy of interchange" with the rest of the charges in the universe suitably averaged; and he satisfied himself that the term must be $\sqrt{\mathcal{N}}/R_E$, apart from a possible numerical factor of order unity, where $\mathcal{N}$ is the number of particles in the universe and R_E is the radius of the initial static Einstein-universe. In this manner, he obtained the relation,

$$(19) \qquad \frac{\sqrt{\mathcal{N}}}{R_E} = \frac{m_e c^2}{e^2}.$$

But we also have the relation (cf. equation 18)

$$\frac{G\mathcal{N}m_p}{c^2} = \tfrac{1}{2}\pi R_E, \qquad (20)$$

where m_p denotes the mass of the proton. From these two relations, we find

$$\mathcal{N} = \frac{\pi^2}{4} \frac{e^4}{(Gm_p m_e)^2} = 1.28 \times 10^{79}$$

and

$$\frac{1}{\Lambda} = R_E = \tfrac{1}{2}\pi \frac{e^4}{Gm_p m_e^2 c^2} = 1.07 \times 10^9 \text{ light years.} \qquad (21)$$

Eddington considered these values to be sufficiently in accord with the observations that he felt that he had detected his "criminal." From this point on, he had no doubts about the soundness of his arguments. Indeed, in a course of lectures he gave at the Institute for Advanced Studies in Dublin in 1943, he stated

> At no time during the past sixteen years have I felt any doubt about the correctness of my theory.[48]

It is now pertinent to ask what the present status of Eddington's cosmological model is. The advances in our knowledge since 1944 leave little doubt that it is not the right one. The evidences derive, principally, from the discovery of the universal 3 K black-body radiation and the fact that helium is of primordial origin.

The fact that the universe is pervaded by a homogeneous isotropic radiation-field with a Planckian distribution at a temperature of 3 K, implies that the universe has expanded by a factor of some 1300 from the time when the temperature of the universal radiation was 4000 K and the decoupling of the matter and the radiation occurred. Similarly, the production of primordial helium by nucleosynthesis implies that the universe, at one time, was in a state in which the density was of the order of 1000 g/cm^3 and the temperature was of the order of 10^9 K. These requirements, in turn, imply that the radius of the universe, at that time, must have been smaller by a factor of the order of 10^9. Variations in the radius of the universe of this magnitude are simply incompatible with Eddington's cosmological model.

On 9 June 1944, barely five months before he died, Eddington, in his last appearance at a meeting of the Royal Astronomical Society, presented a paper on "The Recession-Constant of the Galaxies." On this occasion, Eddington stated that Λ given by equation (21) "*is* the cosmical constant," and further that

> . . . the time scale for the evolution of the universe is definitely less than 90×10^9 years, and I do not see much prospect of evading this limit.[49]

After the presentation of the paper, the following exchange between Eddington and G. C. McVittie took place:

> DR. MCVITTIE: The theory seems to be based entirely on the model which starts expanding from the Einstein universe. It is known that the observations of the distribution of spiral nebulae "in depth" provide a very delicate test for distinguishing between one model universe and another. What becomes of the theory if observation does not happen to select the particular model you have used?
>
> SIR ARTHUR EDDINGTON: I do not think we shall have data accurate enough to settle this point for a very long time, so that I do not think I need consider the contingency! We have to try to reach a conclusion by other means than a direct comparison with observation.[50]

The contingency to which Eddington refers has occurred; and McVittie's question remains unanswered.

XIV

I have already described Eddington's line of argument in relating the number of particles in the universe with atomic constants. For the further development of his theory, he needed to enumerate the number of cells of volume h^3 in the available phase-space of the initial static Einstein-universe. The required enumeration was, in Eddington's mind, closely related to, if not the same as, the enumeration one makes when deriving the equation of state of a degenerate electron-gas consistently with Pauli's exclusion principle. Since I am involved in this matter, I shall read from a detailed statement that Eddington has made of the evolution of his ideas in this regard, in an address to the Tercentenary Conference of Arts and Sciences at Harvard University, in the summer of 1936:

> . . . in the stars the temperature of 10 million degrees causes most of the satellite electrons to be torn away from the atom, and what is left of the atom is a tiny structure. The atoms or ions are so reduced in size that they will not jam until densities 100000 times greater are reached. For this reason, the perfect gas state continues up to much higher densities

in the stars. The sun and other dense stars insisted on obeying the theory worked out for a perfect gas, as they had every right to do, since their material was perfect gas.

There was, therefore, nothing to prevent stellar matter from becoming compressed to exceedingly high density; and it suggested itself that the densities which had been calculated from observation for certain stars called white dwarfs, which had seemed impossibly high, might be genuine after all.

In reaching this conclusion I was not without a certain misgiving. I was uneasy as to what would ultimately happen to these superdense stars. The star seemed to have got itself into an awkward fix. Ultimately its store of subatomic energy would give out and the star would then want to cool down. But could it? The enormous density was made possible by the high temperature which shattered the atoms. If the material cooled it would presumably revert to terrestrial density. But that meant that the star must expand to say 5000 times its present bulk. But the expansion requires energy—doing work against gravity; and the star appeared to have no store of energy available. What on earth was the star to do if it was continually losing heat, but had not enough energy to get cold!

The high density of the companion of Sirius was duly confirmed by Professor Adams—but this puzzle remained. Shortly afterward Prof. R. H. Fowler came to the rescue in a famous paper, in which he applied a new result in wave mechanics which had just been discovered. It is a remarkable coincidence that just at the time when matter of transcendently great density was discovered in astronomy, the mathematical physicists were quite independently turning attention to the same subject. I suppose that up to 1924 no one had given a serious thought to abnormally dense matter; but just when it cropped up in astronomy it cropped up in physics as well. Fowler showed that the newly discovered Fermi-Dirac statistics saved the star from the unfortunate fate which I had feared.

Not content with letting well alone, physicists began to improve on Fowler's formula. They pointed out that in white dwarf conditions the electrons would have speeds approaching the velocity of light, and there would be certain relativity effects which Fowler had neglected. Consequently, Fowler's formula, called the *ordinary* degeneracy formula, came to be superseded by a newer formula, called the *relativistic* degeneracy formula. All seemed well until certain researches by Chandrasekhar brought out the fact that the relativistic formula put the stars back in precisely the same difficulty from which Fowler had rescued them. The small stars could cool down all right, and end their days as dark stars in a reasonable way. But above a certain critical mass (two or three times that of the sun) the star could never cool down, but must go on radiating and contracting until heaven knows what becomes of it. That did not worry Chandrasekhar; he seemed to like the stars to behave that way, and believes that that is what really happens. But I felt the same objections as 12 years earlier to this stellar buffoonery; at least it was sufficiently strange to rouse my suspicion that there must be something wrong with the physical formula used.

I examined the formula—the so-called relativistic degeneracy formula—and the conclusion I came to was that it was the result of a combination of relativity theory with a nonrelativistic quantum theory. I do not regard the offspring of such a union as born in lawful wedlock. The relativistic degeneracy formula—the formula currently used—is in fact baseless; and, perhaps rather surprisingly, the formula derived by a correct application of relativity theory is the ordinary formula—Fowler's original formula which every one had abandoned. I was not surprised to find that in announcing these conclusions I had put my foot in a hornet's nest; and I have had the physicists buzzing about my ears—but I don't think I have been stung yet. Anyhow, for the purposes of this lecture, I will assume that I haven't dropped a brick.

I venture to refer to a personal aspect of this investigation, since it shows how closely different branches of science are interlocked. At the time when my suspicion of the relativistic degeneracy formula was roused by Chandrasekhar's results, it was very inconvenient to me to spare time to follow it up, because I was immersed in a long investigation in a different field of thought. This work, which had occupied me for six years, was nearing completion and there remained only one problem, namely, the accurate theoretical calculation of the cosmical constant, needed to round it off. But there I had completely stuck. I had, however, secured a period of four months free from distractions which I intended to devote to it—to make a supreme effort, so to speak. But having incautiously begun to think about the degeneracy formula I could not get away from it. It took up my time. The months slipped away, and I had done nothing with the problem of the cosmical constant. Then one day in trying to test my degeneracy results from all points of view, I found that in one limiting case it merged into a cosmical problem. It gave a new approach to the very problem which I had had to put aside—and from this new approach the problem was soluble without much difficulty. I can see now that it would have been very difficult to get at it in any other way; and it is most unlikely that I should have made any progress if I had spent the four months on the direct line of attack which I had planned.

The paper which I read to the mathematical section a few days ago, giving a calculation of the speed of recession of the spiral nebulae and the number of particles in the universe, had an astronomical origin. It was not, however, suggested by consideration of the spiral nebulae. It arose out of the study of the companion of Sirius and other white dwarf stars.[51]

Let me explain what the points at issue were. Fowler's discussion of the state of matter in the white-dwarf stars was based on precisely the same theory of the degenerate electron-gas that had been made familiar by Sommerfeld's electron theory of metals. The equation of state governing such an electron gas is

$$p = \frac{1}{20} \left(\frac{3}{\pi}\right)^{2/3} \frac{h^2}{m_e} n^{5/3}, \tag{22}$$

where p denotes the pressure and n the number of electrons per cm³. However, at the densities prevailing at the centers of white-dwarf stars, the electrons at the Fermi threshold begin to have velocities comparable to that of light. If one allows for this circumstance, in a way that was common then and continues to be common to this day, one finds that the equation of state departs from that given by equation (22) and, in the limit of very high electron-concentrations, tends to

$$p = \frac{1}{8} \left(\frac{3}{\pi}\right)^{1/3} hc \, n^{4/3} \qquad (n \to \infty). \tag{23}$$

It is this modification of the equation of state which Eddington considered as "baseless."

The consequences which result from using the equation of state in its nonrelativistic form (22) and in its exact form with the low- and the high-density limits (22) and (23), are the following.

On the basis of the nonrelativistic equation of state (22), one finds that stellar masses, in equilibrium, have radii which vary inversely as the cube root of the mass. Finite equilibrium configurations are, therefore, possible for all masses. It is this fact which Eddington considered as eminently satisfactory. However, when one uses the exact form of the equation of state, with its high-density limit (23), one finds that no equilibrium state is possible if the mass exceeds the limit,

$$M_{\text{limit}} = 0.197 \left(\frac{hc}{G}\right)^{3/2} \frac{1}{(\mu_e H)^2} = 5.76 \, \mu_e^{-2} \, \odot, \tag{24}$$

where μ_e is the mean molecular weight per electron. The complete mass-radius relation[52] that one obtains is illustrated in figure 4.

It is this fact, that no finite degenerate stellar-configurations exist for masses exceeding the limit (24), which Eddington considered as "stellar buffoonery." As he stated in an earlier context,

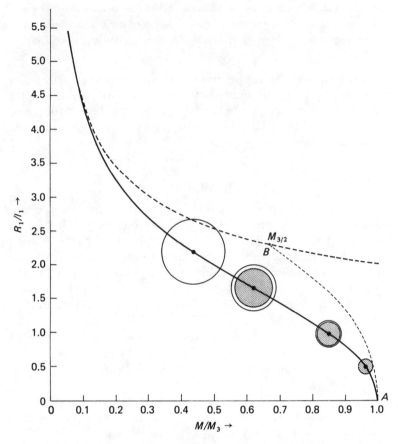

FIG.4 The full-line curve represents the exact (mass–radius) relation for completely degenerate configurations. The mass, along the abscissa, is measured in units of the limiting mass (denoted by M_3) and the radius, along the ordinate, is measured in the unit $l_1 = 7.72\mu^{-1} \times 10^8$ cm. The dashed curve represents the relation that follows from the equation of state (11); at the point B along this curve, the threshold momentum p_0 of the electrons at the center of the configuration is exactly equal to m_ec. Along the exact curve, at the point where a full circle (with no shaded part) is drawn, p_0 (at the center) is again equal to m_ec; the shaded parts of the other circles represent the regions in these configurations where the electrons may be considered to be relativistic ($p_0 > m_ec$). (Reproduced from S. Chandrasekhar, *Mon. Not. Roy. Astr. Soc.* **95**, no. 219 [1935])

Chandrasekhar, using the relativistic formula which has been accepted for the last five years, shows that a star of mass greater than a certain limit $\mathfrak{M}$ remains a perfect gas and can never cool down. The star has to go on radiating and radiating, and contracting and contracting until, I suppose, it gets down to a few km radius, when gravity becomes strong enough to hold in the radiation, and the star can at last find peace.

Dr. Chandrasekhar had got this result before, but he has rubbed it in in his last paper; and, when discussing it with him, I felt driven to the conclusion that this was almost a *reductio ad absurdum* of the relativistic degeneracy formula. Various accidents may intervene to save the star, but I want more protection than that. I think there should be a law of nature to prevent a star from behaving in this absurd way![53]

It is clear from this statement that Eddington fully realized, already in 1935, that given the existence of an upper limit to the mass of degenerate configurations, one must contemplate the possibility of gravitational collapse leading to the formation of what we now call black holes. But he was unwilling to accept a conclusion that he so presciently drew; and he convinced himself that "there should be a law of nature to prevent a star from behaving in this absurd way!"

Again, it is pertinent to ask what the present status of Eddington's convictions with regard to this matter are. The simple and direct answer is that they are not accepted. This is not the occasion, and there is not the time either, to describe how the existence of the limiting mass is inextricably woven into the present fabric of astronomical tapestry with its complex designs of stellar evolution, of nuclear burning in the high-density cores of certain stars, and gravitational collapse leading to the supernova phenomenon and the formation of neutron stars of nearly the same mass and of black holes. All these are discernible even to the most casual observer. For my part I shall only say that I find it hard to understand why Eddington, who was one of the earliest and staunchest supporters of the general theory of relativity, should have found the conclusion that black holes may form during the natural course of the evolution of the stars, so unacceptable. It would appear, then, that two of the main pillars of the grand edifice that Eddington built in his "fundamental theory" have collapsed. Forgetting this fact for a moment, what are we to make of the structure itself? Here are two views.

Eddington's work, if correct, is extremely important, but most of those who have tried to read his work have not been able to agree with his conclusions. His papers are very clear up to a point and then at the critical moment they become obscure, to become clear again after the

important results have been deduced. There is certainly no logical de-
duction of the conclusions from explicitly stated axioms and hypotheses, and Eddington himself was aware of this. Once after a long discussion with the present writer, which achieved very little, Eddington said:
"I can't quite see through the proof, but I am sure the result is correct."
(A. H. Wilson)[54]

Eddington's "unified theory," apart from its obscurity, explains too
much; indeed it explains everything, and hitherto such theories have
generally been found ultimately to explain nothing. At best, it is a frag-
mentary work, which contains flashes of insight that will be appreciated
by future generations, like Leonardo da Vinci's scientific researches,
probably after what is significant in them has been more completely
discovered by very different paths and methods. (J. G. Crowther)[55]

There can, however, be little doubt that, even though Eddington's
edifice may, in part, be in ruins, there are high columns that are still
standing erect. One example must suffice. In his treatment of Dirac's
equation, Eddington developed a calculus of E-numbers which is, ba-
sically, the group algebra of sixteen elements which satisfy the anti-
commutation rules of the Dirac matrices. This development represents
a considerable achievement in itself; and it has had important repercussions in the current renewed interest in Clifford algebras. The basic
elements of Eddington's developments are the following.

Eddington starts by defining five E-numbers by the representation,

$$(25) \quad E_1 = \begin{vmatrix} i\sigma_1 & 0 \\ 0 & i\sigma_1 \end{vmatrix}, E_2 = \begin{vmatrix} i\sigma_3 & 0 \\ 0 & i\sigma_3 \end{vmatrix}, E_3 = \begin{vmatrix} 0 & -\sigma_2 \\ \sigma_2 & 0 \end{vmatrix},$$

$$E_4 = \begin{vmatrix} i\sigma_2 & 0 \\ 0 & -i\sigma_2 \end{vmatrix}, \text{ and } E_5 = \begin{vmatrix} 0 & i\sigma_2 \\ i\sigma_2 & 0 \end{vmatrix},$$

where σ_1, σ_2, and σ_3 are the Pauli 2×2-matrices. These E-numbers
satisfy the commutation rules,

$$(26) \quad E_\mu E_\nu + E_\nu E_\mu = -2\delta_{\mu\nu} \ (\mu, \nu = 1, \ldots, 5),$$

and

$$(27) \quad E_1 E_2 E_3 E_4 = iE_5.$$

And the sixteen elements of Eddington's algebra are

$$(28) \quad i, E_\mu \text{ and } E_\mu E_\nu \ (\mu, \nu = 1, \ldots, 5; \mu \neq \nu).$$

Eddington went further to define the square of the E-algebra as
16×16 complex matrices. This "double E-frame" corresponds to one

of three Clifford albegras in a nine-dimensional base space. Since recent work on super-symmetric gauge-fields is based on eight and nine-dimensional Clifford algebras, Eddington was, in this respect, very much ahead of his time.

Eddington attached considerable importance to finding idempotent E-numbers, i.e., elements E of the algebra satisfying $E^2 = E$. These are the projection operators for momentum and spin in quantum electrodynamics. And finally, his realization that the E-algebra is *five*-dimensional over the real numbers led him to introduce (for the first time in particle physics) the notion of "chirality" derived from the choices, $+i$ or $-i$, on the right-hand side of equation (27). It should also be stated that Eddington was the first to identify the algebra of the 4×4 real matrices and its significance. This algebra was later discovered by E. Majorana; and in the physics literature it is often referred to as the "Majorana spinors."[56]

XVI

I should like to conclude by briefly tracing through Eddington's writings his changing attitude to scientific research. When we juxtapose these attitudes with the directions of his research, we can, perhaps, catch some glimpse of the sources of his strength and of his weakness.

In his address on "The Internal Constitution of the Stars" to the British Association in 1920 (from which I have quoted earlier), Eddington discussed at some length the place of speculation and of idealized models in scientific inquiry. This is what he said:

> . . . I wonder what is the touchstone by which we may test the legitimate development of scientific theory and reject the idly speculative. We all know of theories which the scientific mind instinctively rejects as fruitless guesses; but it is difficult to specify their exact defect or to supply a rule which will show us when we ourselves do err. It is often supposed that to speculate and to make hypotheses are the same thing; but more often they are opposed. It is when we let our thoughts stray outside venerable, but sometimes insecure, hypothesis that we are said to speculate. Hypothesis limits speculation. Moreover, distrust of speculation often serves as a cover for loose thinking—wild ideas take anchorage in our minds and influence our outlook; whilst it is considered too speculative to subject them to the scientific scrutiny which would exorcise them.
>
> If we are not content with the dull accumulation of experimental facts, if we make any deductions or generalizations, if we seek for any theory to guide us, some degree of speculation canot be avoided. Some

will prefer to take the interpretation which seems to be most immediately indicated and at once adopt that as an hypothesis; others will rather seek to explore and classify the widest possibilities which are not definitely inconsistent with the facts. Either choice has its dangers: the first may be too narrow a view and lead progress into a cul-de-sac; the second may be so broad that it is useless as a guide and diverges indefinitely from experimental knowledge. When this last case happens, it must be concluded that the knowledge is not yet ripe for theoretical treatment and speculation is premature. The time when speculative theory and observational research may profitably go hand in hand is when the possibilities—or, at any rate, the probabilities—can be narrowed down by experiment, and the theory can indicate the tests by which the remaining wrong paths may be blocked up one by one.

The mathematical physicist is in a position of peculiar difficulty. He may work out the behaviour of an ideal model of material with specifically defined properties, obeying mathematically exact laws, and so far his work is unimpeachable. It is no more speculative than the binomial theorem. But when he claims a serious interest for his toy, when he suggests that his model is like something going on in nature, he inevitably begins to speculate. Is the actual body really like the ideal model? May not other unknown conditions intervene? He cannot be sure, but he cannot suppress the comparison; for it is by looking continually to nature that he is guided in his choice of a subject. A common fault, to which he must often plead guilty, is to use for the comparison data over which the more experienced observer shakes his head; they are too insecure to build extensively upon. Yet even in this, theory may help observation by showing the kind of data which it is especially important to improve.

I think that the more idle kinds of speculation will be avoided if the investigation is conducted from the right point of view. When the properties of an ideal model have been worked out by rigorous mathematics, all the underlying assumptions being clearly understood, then it becomes possible to say that such and such properties and laws lead precisely to such and such effects. If any other disregarded factors are present, they should now betray themselves when a comparison is made with nature. There is no need for disappointment at the failure of the model to give perfect agreement with observation; it has served its purpose, for it has distinguished what are the features of the actual phenomena which require new conditions for their explanation. A general preliminary agreement with observation is necessary, otherwise the model is hopeless; not that it is necessarily wrong so far as it goes, but it has evidently put the less essential properties foremost. We have been pulling at the wrong end of the tangle, which has to be unravelled by a different approach. But after a general agreement with observation is established, and the tangle begins to loosen, we should always make ready for the next knot. I suppose that the applied mathematician whose theory has just passed one still more stringent test by observation ought not to feel satisfaction, but rather disappointment—"Foiled again! This time I had hoped to find a discordance which would throw light on the points where my model could be improved." Perhaps that is a counsel of perfection; I own that I have never felt very keenly a disappointment of this kind.

Our model of nature should not be like a building—a handsome structure for the populace to admire, until in the course of time someone takes away a corner-stone and the edifice comes toppling down. It should be like an engine with movable parts. We need not fix the position of any one lever—that is to be adjusted from time to time as the latest observations indicate. The aim of the theorist is to know the train of wheels which the lever sets in motion—that binding of the parts which is the soul of the engine.[57]

There is hardly anything in the foregoing statement to which any serious practitioner of theoretical astrophysics will object. Eddington concluded a lecture on "The Source of Stellar Energy" give at this time with the modest appraisal:

> I should have liked to have closed these lectures by leading up to some great climax. But perhaps it is more in accordance with the true conditions of scientific progress that they should fizzle out with a glimpse of the obscurity which marks the frontiers of present knowledge. I do not apologize for the lameness of the conclusion, for it is not a conclusion. I wish I could feel confident that it is even a beginning.[58]

And this is entirely consistent with the approach to scientific inquiry that I have read. A shift in attitude is already discernible in this statement made two years later:

> In science we sometimes have convictions as to the right solution of a problem which we cherish but cannot justify; we are influenced by some innate sense of the fitness of things.[59]

Soon Eddington became cocksure of his views on the cosmical constant, on his cosmological model, on relativistic degeneracy, on the formation of black holes, and, indeed, on his whole approach to "the unification of quantum theory and relativity theory." This is abundantly clear from the various quotations from his writings and his lectures that I have read in these contexts. This radical shift in Eddington's attitude is strikingly illustrated by contrasting the modest appraisal of his work on the internal constitution of the stars in 1926 with the self-assured confidence of the remark that he made to me ten years later:

> . . . You look at it from the point of view of the star; I look at it from the point of view of nature.

Clearly, at this time, Eddington's views no longer had the kind of sureness which was not cocksureness.

In spite of his expressed confidence of the correctness of his fundamental theory, Eddington must have been deeply frustrated by the neglect of his work by his contemporaries. This frustration is expressed in his plaintive letter to Dingle late in 1944:

> I am continually trying to find out why people find the procedure obscure. But I would point out that even Einstein was considered obscure, and hundreds of people have thought it necessary to explain him. I cannot seriously believe that I ever attain the obscurity that Dirac does. But in the case of Einstein and Dirac people have thought it worthwhile to penetrate the obscurity. I believe they will understand me all right when they realize they have got to do so—and when it becomes the fashion "to explain Eddington."[60]

And it is haunting to read

> In his last years, his ghostly pale face was drawn with suffering as he sat in his long reveries.[61]

Perhaps Eddington foresaw the direction of his future scientific inquiries when he narrated the story of Daedalus and Icarus in his British Association Address of 1920:

> In ancient days two aviators procured to themselves wings. Daedalus flew safely through the middle air across the sea, and was duly honoured on his landing. Young Icarus soared upwards towards the Sun till the wax melted which bound his wings, and his flight ended in fiasco. In weighing their achievements perhaps there is something to be said for Icarus. The classic authorities tell us that he was only "doing a stunt," but I like to think of him as the man who certainly brought to light a constructional defect in the flying machines of his day. So, too, in Science, cautious Daedalus will apply his theories where he feels most confident they will safely go; but by his excess of caution their hidden weaknesses cannot be brought to light. Icarus will strain his theories to the breaking-point till the weak joints gape. For a spectacular stunt? Perhaps partly; he is often very human. But if he is not yet destined to reach the Sun and solve for all time the riddle of its constitution, yet we

may hope to learn from his journey some hints to build a better machine.[62]

And so today, we remember with reverence a great spirit that soared undaunted towards the sun.

NOTES

1. *Astrophys. J.* **101**, 133 (1945).

2. A. Vibert Douglas, *The Life of Arthur Stanley Eddington* (London: Thomas Nelson & Sons, 1957), p. 103.

3. A. S. Eddington, *Stars and Atoms* (Oxford: Clarendon Press, 1927), p. 24; and J. G. Crowther, *British Scientists of the Twentieth Century,* chap. 4 (London: Routledge & Kegan Paul, 1952), p. 177.

4. A. S. Eddington, *New Pathways in Science* (Cambridge: Cambridge University Press, 1935), p. 207.

5. *New Pathways in Science,* p. 170.

6. A. S. Eddington, *Science and the Unseen World* (London: Allen & Unwin, 1929), p. 33.

7. *Science and the Unseen World,* pp. 54–56.

8. A. S. Eddington, "Forty Years of Astronomy," in *Background to Modern Science,* ed. J. Needham and W. Pagel (Cambridge: Cambridge University Press, 1938), pp. 120–21.

9. A. S. Eddington, *Internal Constitution of the Stars* (Cambridge: Cambridge University Press), pp. 15–16, 245.

10. *Observatory* **43**, 353–55 (1920).

11. *Nature,* 1 May 1926 (supplement), no. 2948, p. 30.

12. *Astrophys. J.* **101**, 134 (1945).

13. *Observatory* **52**, 349 (1929).

14. *Observatory* **49**, 250, 335 (1926).

15. *Observatory* **40**, 224–26 (1917).

16. *Notes & Records Roy. Soc. London* **30**, 249 (1976).

17. A. S. Eddington, *Space, Time and Gravitation* (Cambridge: Cambridge University Press, 1920), pp. 113–14.

18. "Forty Years of Astronomy," pp. 140–42.

19. *Mon. Not. Roy. Astr. Soc.* **85**, 672 (1924–25).

20. *Observatory* **42**, 389–98 (1919).

21. *Observatory* **55**, 5 (1932).

22. *Observatory* **46**, 142 (1923).

23. *New Pathways in Science,* p. 121.

24. *Math. Gazette* **19**, 256–57 (1935).

25. More generally, if A, B, C, and D speak the truth with probabilities a, b, c, and d, respectively, then the solution of the same problem, as L. S. Leftwich showed in considerable detail (*Math. Gazette* **20**, 309–10 [1936]), is:

$$\frac{d - acd(1 - b)}{1 - a(1 - b) + a(1 - b)(c - 2cd + d)}$$

26. A. S. Eddington, *Mathematical Theory of Relativity* (Cambridge: Cambridge University Press, 1923), p. 10.

27. *Observatory* **46**, 193 (1923).

28. *Nature* **113**, 192 (1924).

29. *Proc. Roy. Soc. (Lond.)* **A102**, 268 (1922).

30. *Proc. Roy. Soc. (Lond.)* **A166**, 465 (1938).

31. *The Life of Arthur Stanley Eddington,* pp. 189–92.

32. *Mathematical Theory of Relativity,* p. 153.

33. Ibid., p. 154.

34. Ibid., p. 155.

35. A. S. Eddington, *The Expanding Universe* (Cambridge: Cambridge University Press, 1933), p. 35.

36. *New Pathways in Science,* p. 315.

37. *The Expanding Universe,* pp. 147–48.

38. *Einstein: A Centenary Volume,* ed. A. P. French (Cambridge, Mass.: Harvard University Press, 1979), p. 274.

39. *The Life of Arthur Stanley Eddington,* p. 57.

40. *Proc. Nat. Acad. Sci.* **18**, 213 (1932).

41. "Forty Years of Astronomy," p. 128.

42. W. Pauli, *Theory of Relativity,* trans. G. Field (London: Pergamon Press, 1958), p. 220.

43. W. Rindler, *Essential Relativity* (Berlin: Springer-Verlag, 1977), p. 226.

44. *Records of R.A.S. Club 1925–1953,* ed. G. J. Whitrow, pp. xxiv–xxvii.

45. I am excluding the nonstatic solutions discovered by Freidmann in 1922 since they came to be known generally only several years later.

46. *Proc. Phys. Soc.* **44**, 6 (1932).

47. *The Expanding Universe,* p. 87.

48. *Dublin Inst. Adv. Studies* **A2**, 1 (1943).

49. *Observatory* **65**, 211 (1944).

50. Ibid., p. 212.

51. *Ann. Rep. Smithsonian Institution* (Washington, D.C.: U.S. Government Printing Office, 1938), pp. 137–39.

52. *Mon. Not. R. Astr. Soc.* **95**, 207 (1935).

53. *Observatory* **58**, 37 (1935).

54. *Cambridge Review* **66**, 171 (1945).

55. *British Scientists,* p. 195.

56. I am greatly indebted to Dr. N. Salingaros for drawing my attention to the significance and the importance of Eddington's work on his *E*-numbers.

57. *Observatory* **43**, 356–57 (1920).

58. *Nature,* 1 May 1926 (supplement), no. 2948, p. 32.

59. A. S. Eddington, *The Nature of the Physical World* (Cambridge: Cambridge University Press, 1928), p. 337.

60. *British Scientists,* p. 194.

61. Ibid., p. 143.

62. *Observatory* **43**, 357–58 (1920).

Stellar Movements and the Structure of the Universe (London: Macmillan & Co., 1914).

Report on the Relativity Theory of Gravitation (London: Physical Society, 1915).

Relativity Theory of Protons and Electrons (Cambridge: Cambridge University Press, 1936).

Fundamental Theory (Cambridge: Cambridge University Press, 1946).

7

KARL SCHWARZSCHILD LECTURE

The Aesthetic Base of the General Theory of Relativity

I

Karl Schwarzschild is, of course, one of the towering physical scientists of this century. The breadth and range of his contributions are staggering: they cover the entire range of physics, astronomy, and astrophysics of his time.

In physics, they range from electrodynamics and geometrical optics to the then newly developing atomic theory of Bohr and Sommerfeld. In electrodynamics, he derived a variational base for Lorentz's equations of the electron. In geometrical optics, he developed the theory of the aberrations in optical instruments (described by Max Born as "unsurpassed in clarity and rigour by later work") and formulated the principle underlying the optics of the Schmidt telescope. And in the Bohr-Sommerfeld theory, he worked out, in his last published paper, the theory of the Stark effect and of the Deslander term in the rotational-vibrational spectra of diatomic molecules. (In this last paper he introduced, for the first time, the notions of action and angle variables.)

In astronomy and astrophysics, Schwarzschild's contributions are so many and so varied that I shall mention only those of his discoveries to which his name is attached. We have the Schwarzschild exponent in photographic photometry, the Schwarzschild-Milne integral equation in the theory of radiative transfer, the Schwarzschild criterion for the

This lecture in memory of Karl Schwarzschild was given at the Astronomischen Gesellschaft in Hamburg, West Germany, on 18 September 1986. It was published in *Mitteilungen der Astronomische Gesellschaft* Nr. 67, Hamburg (1986), and is reprinted here with permission.

onset of convective instability, the Schwarzschild ellipsoidal distribution of stellar velocities, and, of course, the Schwarzschild solution of Einstein's equations for describing the space-time external to a spherical distribution of mass and of static black-holes. And all of these in a brief twenty years!

It is possible that the announced title of my lecture has puzzled some of you: it is not addressed to any concrete topic as the earlier lectures in this series have been; and I am afraid that it will scarcely have any astronomical overtone. My lecture, however, will bear on Schwarzschild's attitude and approach to scientific problems, as I can discern them from his published papers; and it will bear very directly on his solution of the equations of general relativity.

II

I shall consider three examples from Schwarzschild's work which, to my mind, illustrate his approach to scientific problems.

The first relates to his work on star-streaming. The phenomenon was discovered by J. C. Kapteyn; and it was adequately interpreted, almost at once, by Eddington on the basis of his and Kapteyn's hypothesis of two star-streams. Schwarzschild expressed his reaction to this hypothesis as follows *:

> The magnitudes of the proper motions of the stars in the two streams and along with them, presumably also, their average distances from the sun would appear to be equal. The stars in the two streams, during their motion through each other, must, therefore, share common fluctuations; and it is problematical how this can be brought about.
>
> I have, therefore, believed that the same observational material on which Eddington has based himself should be reworked on a more unified hypothesis concerning stellar motions.

On these grounds, Schwarzschild formulated his ellipsoidal distribution of the peculiar velocities of stars; and this formulation has been the basis of all subsequent discussions bearing on stellar motions and the dynamics of stellar systems. What is remarkable to me, however, is his argument: a description of nature must be natural; it cannot be *ad hoc*.

As a second example, I shall take a still earlier publication of Schwarzschild. At a meeting of this Gesellschaft in 1900, Schwarzschild addressed himself to the question whether the geometry of the

* This and the other translations from German of the originals (including Einstein's "Gedächtnisrede" in the appendix) are the author's.

three-dimensional space of astronomy might be non-Euclidean. He stated the problem as follows.

> As must be known to you, during this century [meaning the nineteenth century] one has developed non-Euclidean geometry (besides Euclidean geometry), the chief examples of which are the so-called spherical and pseudo-spherical spaces. We can wonder how the world would appear in a spherical or a pseudo-spherical geometry with possibly a finite radius of curvature. . . . One would then find oneself, if one will, in a geometrical fairyland; and one does not know whether the beauty of this fairyland may not in fact be realized in nature.

We can only marvel at Schwarzschild's scientific imagination and curiosity in addressing himself to such a question some fifteen years before the founding of general relativity. But to Schwarzschild, it was more than simple imagination. He actually estimated limits to the radius of curvature of the three-dimensional space with the astronomical data available at his time and concluded that if the space is hyperbolic its radius of curvature cannot be less than 64 light years and that if the space is spherical its radius of curvature must at least be 1600 light years.

We need not argue about Schwarzschild's particular estimates. It is far more relevant that Schwarzschild allowed his imagination to contemplate a world that may have features of a fairyland!

My third example bears on Schwarzschild's discovery of the solution of Einstein's vacuum-equations appropriate to the exterior of a central spherical distribution of mass—undoubtedly the most important discovery in relativity after its founding.

Schwarzschild's paper in which he derived his solution was communicated by Einstein to the Berlin Academy on 13 January 1916, just about two months after Einstein himself had published the basic equations of his theory in a short communication—his detailed paper with full derivations was still six months in the future—and had deduced the theoretical rate of the precession of the perihelion of Mercury and of the magnitude of the deflection a light ray will experience as it grazes the limb of the sun. In acknowledging Schwarzschild's paper, Einstein wrote on 9 January 1916,

> I have read your paper with greatest interest. I had not expected that one could obtain the exact solution of the problem so simply. The analytical treatment of the problem appears to me splendid.

The circumstances under which Schwarzschild derived his now famous solution were heroic. During the spring and summer of 1915, Schwarzschild was serving in the German army at the eastern front.

While at the eastern front with a small technical staff, Schwarzschild contracted pemphigus, a fatal disease; and he died on 11 May 1916. It was during this period of illness that Schwarzschild wrote his two papers on general relativity—the second one dealt with the equilibrium of a homogeneous mass and showed that no hydrostatic equilibrium is possible if the radius of the object is less than 9/8 of the Schwarzschild radius, $2GM/c^2$—and the fundamental one on the Bohr-Sommerfeld theory to which I have already referred.

About Schwarzschild's last illness, Eddington wrote in a moving obituary notice:

> His end is a sad story of long suffering from a terrible illness contracted in the field, borne with great courage and patience.

Parenthetically, I may add a footnote. Richard Courant told me in the late thirties that he had met Karl Schwarzschild proceeding to the eastern front while he, as a member of the general staff, was with a party retreating from the same front; and Courant said that he was surprised that someone as distinguished as Karl Schwarzschild would be proceeding towards a front that was considered too dangerous for the general staff!

Let me return to Schwarzschild's original paper and his reasons for seeking an exact solution to the problem which Einstein had solved earlier by an approximate procedure. Schwarzschild began with the statement:

> It is always satisfying to obtain an exact solution in a simple form. It is even more important, in the present instance, to have the uniqueness of the solution established and remove whatever doubts there may be concerning Mr. Einstein's treatment of the problem, since, as it will appear below, it is difficult, in the nature of this problem, to establish the validity of an approximate procedure.

While Einstein in his letter of acknowledgement to Schwarzschild (quoted earlier) argued that there can be no doubts about the validity of his approximate procedure in solving the equations, it is significant that Schwarzschild, undaunted, wished to solve exactly the problem which he realized was a fundamental one in the newly formulated theory. I said "undaunted" in view of the great much-ado that was to be made soon afterwards (and for some decades, to the detriment of the theory) about the "difficulty" of Einstein's theory in general and of finding exact solutions in particular.

I shall return later to the role of exact solutions for the understanding of general relativity. But I must pass on now to the main subject of my lecture.

The general theory of relativity has often been described as an extremely beautiful theory; it has even been compared to a work of art (by Rutherford and by Max Born, for example). In the same vein, statements like the following ones by Dirac are not uncommon:

> What makes the theory so acceptable to physicists, in spite of its going against the principle of simplicity, is its great *mathematical beauty*. (1939)

> The Einstein theory of gravitation has a character of excellence of its own. (1978)

These and similar characterizations of the general theory of relativity raise the following questions:

What is the aesthetic base of the theory? And, more importantly, to what extent is an aesthetic sensibility to its excellence relevant to the formulation and solution of problems which will lead to a deeper understanding of the theory?

To answer these questions without descending to dilettantism, it is first necessary to appreciate the present peculiar position of the general theory of relativity with respect to its confirmation by observation and experiment; and the reasons for its inspiring confidence in spite of inadequate empirical support.

During the past twenty years a great deal of commendable effort has been expended to verify the lowest first-order departures from the Newtonian theory that the general theory of relativity predicts. These efforts have been successful and the predictions of the theory relating to the differing rates of time-keeping in locations of differing gravity; to the deflection a light ray experiences when traversing a gravitational field and the consequent time delay; to the precession of a Kepler orbit; and, finally, to the slowing down of the orbital period of a binary star in an eccentric orbit by virtue of the emission of gravitational radiation, have all been confirmed within the limits of observational and experimental errors and uncertainties. But all these effects relate to departures from the predictions of the Newtonian theory by a few parts in a million, and of no more than three or four parameters in a post-Newtonian expansion of the Einstein field-equations. And, so far, *no* predictions of general relativity, in the limit of strong gravitational fields, have received any confirmation; and none seem likely in the foreseeable future.

Should one not argue that a confirmation of a theory, which generalizes a theory as well tested in its domain of validity as the Newtonian theory, should refer to predictions which relate to major aspects of the theory, rather than to small first-order departures from the theory which it replaces? Would the status of Dirac's theory of the electron, for example, be what it is today if its only success consisted in accounting for Paschen's 1916 measurements of the fine-structure splittings of the lines of ionized helium? The real confirmation of Dirac's theory that inspired confidence was the discovery, in accordance with the theory, of electron-positron pairs in cosmic-ray showers. Similarly, would our faith in Maxwell's equations of the electromagnetic field be as universal as it is without Hertz's experiments on the propagation of electromagnetic waves with precisely the velocity of light *and* without Poincaré's proof of their invariance to Lorentz transformations? In the same way, a real confirmation of the general theory of relativity will be forthcoming only if a prediction characteristic of the theory, and only of that theory, is confirmed. The occurrence of black holes as one of the final equilibrium states of massive stars in the natural course of their evolution is not a confirmation of a prediction of general relativity in any real sense. The notion that light cannot escape from a sufficiently strong gravitational field is an inference not based on any exact prediction of the theory; it depends only on the empirical fact that light is affected by gravity. On the other hand, since the general theory of relativity provides an exact description of the space-time around black holes, only a confirmation of the metric of the space-time around black holes can be considered as "establishing" the theory in any real sense. It is well known that the Kerr solution with two parameters provides the unique solution for stationary black-holes that can occur in the astronomical universe. But a confirmation of the metric of the Kerr space-time (or some aspect of it) cannot even be contemplated in the foreseeable future.

Perhaps, I may digress here to indicate how one may eventually have a confirmation of the space-time around a rotating Kerr black-hole. If one imagines a Kerr black-hole with an accretion disc of free electrons in the equatorial plane, then the polarization of the light emerging from it, after traversing the strong gravitational field of the black hole, will manifest so nonuniform a distribution that one should be able to map it. Will Nature be generous enough to provide a clean example which will enable such a mapping? I am afraid that this is the only time my talk will bear on an astronomical observation.

IV

As I have said, we have, as yet, no exact feature of general relativity that has been confirmed by observation; and none appears feasible in the foreseeable future. Why then do we have faith and confidence in the theory? One should respond more explicitly than merely to say, as some have, that our confidence derives from the "beauty of the mathematical description of Nature which the theory provides."

> To the solid ground of Nature trusts the mind that builds for aye!

So said Wordsworth. There is no solid ground for the general theory of relativity. On what then do we build our trust? We build our trust on the internal consistency of the theory and on its conformity with what we believe are general physical requirements; and, above all, on its freedom from contradiction with parts of physics not contemplated in the formulation of the theory. Let me illustrate by some examples.

The causal character of the laws of physics requires that, given complete initial data on a space-like three-surface, the future is uniquely determined in the space-time domain bounded by the future-directed in-going null rays emanating from the boundary of the spatial slice. More formally stated: the basic equations of any physical theory must allow an initial-value formulation which determines uniquely the future development in the entire domain of dependence of the initial data on a spatial slice. The field equations of general relativity do allow such a formulation, though the proof of this fact is not straightforward: it was provided only in 1944 by Lichnerowicz.

As a second example, consider the notion of energy that is so central to physics. In physics, one is accustomed to define a local energy that is globally conserved. The fact that an isolated body which is not static or stationary will emit gravitational waves that contribute to the energy, implies that in general relativity we cannot expect to have a local definition of energy. But one should expect that, if space-time is asymptotically flat (in some well-defined sense), one should be able to define, globally, for the entire space (extending to infinity) a total energy that is positive. In 1962, Bondi was able to show that if the space-time is asymptotically flat at null-infinity (i.e., as we go to infinity along null-rays), then one can define a mass-function—the Bondi mass—that is a decreasing function of time; and, further, that the rate of decrease of this mass-function is exactly equal to the rate at which energy is radiated to infinity in the form of gravitational waves. But a proof that the Bondi mass always remains positive finally emerged only in recent years (Schoen and Yau 1981; Witten 1981; and Horowitz and Perry 1982). The proof requires that the energy-momentum tensor, T_{ij}, satisfy some "energy conditions." For a perfect fluid, for which

$$T_{ij} = (\epsilon + p)\, u_i u_j - p g_{ij},$$

the required conditions are equivalent to

$$\epsilon \geq |p|.$$

The foregoing two examples, deep in the structure of the general theory of relativity, illustrate its internal consistency—a consistency by no means obvious or self-evident.

An even more remarkable feature of the general theory of relativity is that it does not violate the laws of other branches of physics not contemplated in its formulation, such as thermodynamics or quantum theory, so long as one does not transgress the domain of validity of the theory. (I shall return presently to the meaning I attach to the phrase "the domain of validity of the general theory of relativity.")

My first example derives from a consideration of the behavior of electron waves, described by Dirac's equation, in the space-time of a Kerr black-hole. It is known that one can extract the rotational energy of the black hole by processes which result in the slowing down of its rotation. More precisely, if we have waves, with a time (t) and an azimuthal-angle (ϕ) dependence given by

$$e^{i(\sigma t + m\phi)} \ (m = 0, \ \pm 1, \ \pm 2, \ \dots \ ),$$

with a frequency σ (>0) less than the critical value

$$\sigma_s = -am/2Mr_+ \ (m = -1, \ -2, \ \dots \ ),$$

where a and M are the Kerr parameters and r_+ is the radius of the event horizon, then one has super-radiance (by which one means that the reflection coefficient for the incident waves exceeds unity). This super-radiance is a necessary consequence of a theorem due to Hawking that every interaction of a black hole with an external source must always result in an increase of the surface area of the event horizon provided only that the energy-momentum tensor of the external source is compatible with the positive-definite character of the energy. However, when one considers the reflection of Dirac waves by the Kerr black-hole, one finds, by a well-defined mathematical algorism of the theory, that they do *not* exhibit the phenomenon of super-radiance. Apparently, then, Hawking's theorem is violated. But one soon realizes that the energy-momentum tensor of the Dirac waves, provided by the quantum theory, does not satisfy the positive-energy requirement. Had the standard algorism predicted super-radiance, we should have had a contradiction between the premises of the general theory of relativity and the premises of the quantum theory. But no such contradiction occurs!

Let me consider a second example. Hawking showed in 1975 that, when one considers the curvature of space-time as providing a classical potential for electron (or photon) scattering according to the rules of the quantum theory, one must observe, from the event horizon of a black hole, an emission of electrons (or photons) with a Fermi (or a Planck) distribution at a temperature determined by the constant surface-gravity of the event horizon. Associated with this temperature and the rate at which energy is lost by the emission of the particles, one can define, formally, an entropy. When one pursues this line of reasoning, one finds that the notion of entropy one derives is entirely consistent with all the known laws of thermodynamics and of statistical mechanics. Thermodynamics and statistical mechanics were not contemplated in the formulation of the general theory of relativity; and yet the consequences that follow from the theory do not violate the laws of thermodynamics and of statistical mechanics.

The foregoing illustrations disclose not only the internal consistency of the general theory but also its consistency with the entire domain of physics outside the realm originally contemplated. These are probably sufficient grounds for one's confidence and faith in Einstein's general theory of relativity.

V

There is another feature of the theory that is related to its aesthetic base.

Every valid physical theory is circumscribed by limitations inherent to it. Thus, the Newtonian theory of gravity is limited by the requirement that bodies should be moving with velocities small compared to that of light. The classical laws of mechanics and of electrodynamics are similarly limited by the requirement that the relevant actions are large compared to Planck's quantum of action, h. Likewise, we may expect the general theory of relativity to be limited by the requirement that the intervals of time and of distance are large compared to the Planck scales, $(\hbar G/c^5)^{1/2}$ ($\sim 5.4 \times 10^{-44}$ sec) and $(\hbar G/c^3)^{1/2}$ ($\sim 1.6 \times 10^{-33}$cm), respectively ($\hbar = h/2\pi$).

Any physical theory, which replaces an earlier theory by overcoming its limitations, will envisage circumstances that are peculiar to the theory and whose exact description will provide a basis for its confirmation. In the Newtonian theory of gravitation, the solution to the two-body problem provides an example: its exact solution provides a quantitative explanation for Kepler's laws. Similarly, Bohr's theory of one-electron systems provides an exact derivation of Balmer's formula and an exact basis for determining the ratio of the masses of the electron and the nucleus from the departures of the Pickering series of ionized helium from the Balmer series of hydrogen.

We now ask: what is the essentially new feature of the general theory of relativity? And what are the circumstances which will reveal those features unambiguously?

The essential features of the general theory of relativity are the precise notions regarding space and time which it incorporates. These notions generalize, in magisterial fashion, those that underlie the special theory of relativity. We ask: are there physical circumstances in which these new notions of the theory are manifested in their pristine purity? The space-time around black holes provides the requisite arena. The general theory of relativity solves the problem of these space-times with magnificent completeness. The space-time around black holes is uniquely specified: it is simple and it involves only two parameters: the mass of the black hole and the angular momentum of the black hole; and the behavior in the space-time of all known test particles is exactly predicted. None of the physical theories that have been explored hitherto provides a problem so characteristic of itself and a solution so complete. This feature of the general theory of relativity appears to me as one of its most aesthetically satisfying aspects; and this leads me to examine, more generally, the aesthetic base of the theory.

To examine a physical theory and to state the source of its aesthetic appeal is beset with difficulties. Like all discussions relating to beauty, it is subject to the tastes and the temperaments of the individuals; and it is difficult, if not impossible, to achieve objectivity. Nevertheless, it seems to me that the question is relevant: as a practitioner of the general theory of relativity for the past twenty and more years, I can ask myself: what aspects of the theory appeal to my aesthetic sensibility and how do the aesthetic ingredients of the theory influence and direct the formulation and solution of problems that lead to a deeper understanding of the physical and the mathematical content of the theory?

I have already referred to the theory of the black holes. It is a remarkable fact, to which I have also made reference, that the general theory of relativity provides, for isolated stationary black-holes, a unique solution with just two parameters. As I have said on another occasion,

Black holes are macroscopic objects with masses varying from a few solar masses to millions of solar masses. To the extent they may be considered as stationary and isolated, to that extent, they are all, every single one of them, described *exactly* by the Kerr solution. This is the only instance we have of an exact description of a macroscopic object. Macroscopic objects, as we see them all around us, are governed by a variety of forces, derived from a variety of approximations to a variety of physical theories. In contrast, the only elements in the construction of black holes are our basic concepts of space and time. They are, thus, almost by definition, the most perfect macroscopic objects there are in the universe. And since the general theory of relativity provides a single unique two-parameter family of solutions for their description, they are the simplest objects as well.

But that is not all! Contrary to every prior expectation, the standard equations of mathematical physics, relating to the propagation and scattering of electromagnetic, gravitational, and the Dirac-electron waves, as well as the geodesic equations of particles and of polarized photons, all of them, can be separated and solved exactly. The manner of separation of these equations has led to a reexamination of the century-old problem of the circumstances when partial differential equations in two variables can be separated and solved; and a rich mathematical theory has arisen. As an example, I may refer to the separation of Dirac's spinor-equation of the electron in Kerr geometry. As a corollary, it led to the separation of Dirac's spinor-equation in spheroidal coordinates in Minkowski geometry of special relativity—a separation that had been considered impossible before.

VI

I now turn to the most difficult question to which I wish to address myself, namely, how sensitiveness to the mathematically aesthetic aspects of the theory enables the formulation and solution of problems of physical significance. In answering this question, I should be precise if I am not to descend to dilettantism. That, I am afraid, will require a somewhat more technical language than I have used so far.

There are two major areas in the mathematical theory of relativity in which progress has been made in recent years: the mathematical theory of black holes and the mathematical theory of colliding waves. Black holes, as resulting from the gravitational collapse of massive stars in the late stages of stellar evolution, are well known. But the relevance of the theory bearing on the collision or scattering of waves by waves in general relativity requires explanation.

In the general theory of relativity one can construct plane-fronted gravitational waves confined between two parallel planes with a finite energy per unit area; and, therefore, we can, in the limit, construct impulsive gravitational waves with a δ-function energy-profile. I may parenthetically note that one cannot construct such impulsive waves in electrodynamics. For, a δ-function profile of the energy will imply a square root of a δ-function profile for the field variables; and the square root of a δ-function is simply not permissible for physical description.

In 1971, Khan and Penrose considered the collision of two impulsive gravitational waves with parallel polarizations. They showed that the result of the collision is the development of a space-time singularity not unlike the singularity in the interior of black holes with which we are acquainted. This phenomenon is not manifested in any linearized version of the theory: the occurrence of the singularity, by a focusing of the colliding waves, in no way depends on the amplitude of the waves. Clearly, in this context, nothing short of an exact solution of the problem will suffice to disclose the new phenomenon. In any event, the occurrence of a singularity in this example suggested to Penrose that a new realm in the physics of general relativity remained for exploration. However, there was no substantial progress in this area before one realized that the mathematical theory of black holes is structurally very closely related to the mathematical theory of colliding waves. This fact is, in itself, surprising: one should not have thought that two theories dealing with such disparate physical circumstances would be as closely related as they are. Indeed, by developing the mathematical theory of colliding waves with a view to constructing a mathematical structure architecturally similar to the mathematical theory of black holes, one finds that a variety of new physical implications of the theory emerge—implications one simply could not have foreseen.

VII

A description of how the development to which I have referred was accomplished is not possible without some familiarity with the language of general relativity, any more than an analysis of a musical composition is possible without some familiarity with musical notation.

We are concerned with space-times that describe stationary axisymmetric black-holes and space-times that describe the collision and scattering of plane-fronted waves. In the former case, the metric coefficients are independent of the time, t, and of the azimuthal angle, ϕ, about the axis of rotation; they depend only on the two remaining spatial coordinates, a radial coordinate r and the polar angle θ. In the latter case, the metric coefficients are independent of two space-like coordinates, x^1 and x^2, both ranging from $+\infty$ to $-\infty$; they depend only on the time, t, and the remaining spatial coordinate, x^3, normal to the (x^1, x^2)-planes.

It can be shown that the metric appropriate to a description of stationary axisymmetric black-holes can be written in the form,

(1) $\quad ds^2 = \sqrt{(\Delta\delta)}\left[\chi(dt)^2 - \frac{1}{\chi}(d\phi - \omega dt)^2 \right]$

$$- e^{\mu_2 + \mu_3} \sqrt{\Delta}\left[\frac{(d\eta)^2}{\Delta} + \frac{(d\mu)^2}{\delta} \right],$$

where

(2) $\qquad \Delta = \eta^2 - 1, \; \delta = 1 - \mu^2 = \text{Sin}^2\theta \qquad (\mu = \text{Cos}\theta),$

η is a radial coordinate (measured in a suitable unit), and χ, ω, and $\mu_2 + \mu_3$ are metric functions to be determined. It may be noted, that ω is directly related to the angular momentum of the black hole; it is zero for the Schwarzschild black-hole which is static.

In writing the metric in the form (1), we have already arranged for the occurrence, at $\eta = 1$, of a null surface that will eventually be identified with the event horizon of the black hole.

The central problem of the theory is to solve for χ and ω: once one has solved for them, the remaining metric function, $\mu_2 + \mu_3$, follows by a simple quadrature.

Associated with the metric (1), we have a "conjugate metric" obtained by the transformation,

(3) $\qquad\qquad\qquad t \rightarrow +i\phi \text{ and } \phi \rightarrow -it.$

By this "conjugation," χ and ω are replaced by

(4) $\qquad\qquad \tilde{\chi} = \frac{\chi}{\chi^2 - \omega^2} \text{ and } \tilde{\omega} = \frac{\omega}{\chi^2 - \omega^2}.$

For the solution of the physical problems, it is essential that we consider, in place of χ and ω, the pair of functions, Ψ and Φ, where

(5) $\qquad\qquad\qquad \Psi = \frac{\sqrt{(\Delta\delta)}}{\chi},$

and Φ is a potential for ω defined by

(6) $\qquad\qquad \Phi_{,\eta} = \frac{\delta}{\chi^2}\,\omega_{,\mu} \text{ and } \Phi_{,\mu} = -\frac{\Delta}{\chi^2}\,\omega_{,\eta}.$

One can similarly define $\tilde{\Psi}$ and $\tilde{\Phi}$ in terms $\tilde{\chi}$ and $\tilde{\omega}$.

In the mathematical theory of black holes, one combines the functions Ψ and Φ and $\tilde{\Psi}$ and $\tilde{\Phi}$ into the pairs of complex functions,

$$Z^\dagger = \Psi + i\Phi \text{ and } \tilde{Z}^\dagger = \tilde{\Psi} + i\tilde{\Phi}, \tag{7}$$

and defines

$$E^\dagger = \frac{Z^\dagger - 1}{Z^\dagger + 1} \text{ and } \tilde{E}^\dagger = \frac{\tilde{Z}^\dagger - 1}{\tilde{Z}^\dagger - 1}. \tag{8}$$

Both these functions satisfy the Ernst equation,

$$(1 - |E|^2) \{[(1-\eta^2)E,_\eta],_\eta - [(1-\mu^2)E,_\mu],_\mu\}$$
$$= -2E^*[(1-\eta^2)(E,_\eta)^2 - (1-\mu^2)(E,_\mu)^2]. \tag{9}$$

Turning next to space-times appropriate to the description of colliding waves, we envisage the collision of two plane-fronted impulsive gravitational waves accompanied, in general, with gravitational and other shock-waves with the same fronts, approaching each other from $+\infty$ and $-\infty$. Prior to the instant of collision, the space-time between the approaching wave-fronts is flat. We are principally concerned with the space-time that develops after the instant of collision (though satisfying the boundary conditions at the collision fronts is not a negligible part of the problem).

The metric of the space-time after the instant of collision can be written in the form,

$$ds^2 = -\sqrt{(\Delta\delta)} \left[\chi(dx^2)^2 + \frac{1}{\chi}(dx^1 - q_2 dx^2)^2 \right]$$
$$+ e^{\nu + \mu_3}\sqrt{\Delta}\left[\frac{(d\eta)^2}{\Delta} - \frac{(d\mu)^2}{\delta} \right], \tag{10}$$

where, now,

$$\Delta = 1 - \eta^2, \ \delta = 1 - \mu^2, \tag{11}$$

η measures the time (in a suitable unit) from the instant of collision, μ measures the distance normal to the colliding fronts at the instant of the collision, and χ, q_2, and $\nu + \mu_3$ are metric functions to be determined. It may be noted that q_2 is directly related to the varying plane of polarization of the gravitational waves: it is zero when the plane of polarization is unchanging.

In writing the metric in the form (10), we have taken into account, *a posteriori*, the fact that, as a result of the collision, a curvature or a coordinate singularity develops when $\eta = 1$ and $\mu = \pm 1$.

As in the case of stationary axisymmetric space-times, the solution to the Einstein field-equations can be completed once we have solved for the metric functions χ and q_2 or, equivalently, for Ψ and Φ related to χ and q_2 by

$$(12) \qquad \Psi = \frac{\sqrt{(\Delta\delta)}}{\chi},$$

and

$$(13) \qquad \Phi,_\eta = \frac{\delta}{\chi^2}\, q_{2,\mu} \text{ and } \Phi,_\mu = \frac{\Delta}{\chi^2}\, q_{2,\eta}.$$

In the present case, we need not consider the process of "conjugation" since it corresponds to a simple interchange of the roles of x^1 and x^2.

We now combine the functions χ and q_2 and Ψ and Φ into the pair of complex functions,

$$(14) \qquad Z = \chi + iq_2 \text{ and } Z^\dagger = \Psi + i\Phi,$$

and define

$$(15) \qquad E = \frac{Z - 1}{Z + 1} \text{ and } E^\dagger = \frac{Z^\dagger - 1}{Z^\dagger + 1}.$$

We find that *both* E and $E^\dagger$ satisfy the same Ernst equation (9).

When we turn to the consideration of charged black-holes or the collision of gravitational waves coupled with electromagnetic waves, we must supplement Einstein's equations with Maxwell's equations. For space-times with the two symmetries we are considering, the Maxwell field can be expressed in terms of a single complex-potential $H;$ and the entire set of equations governing the problem can eventually be reduced to a pair of coupled equations for

$$(16) \qquad H \text{ and } Z^\dagger = \Psi + i\Phi + |H|^2,$$

where Ψ is defined as in equations (5) and (12), and Φ is a potential for ω or q_2, defined similarly as in equations (6) and (13) but including additional terms in H on the right-hand sides.

There are two cases when the pair of equations governing $Z^\dagger$ and H can be reduced to a single Ernst equation. These are:

$$(17) \qquad \text{Case (i):} \qquad H = Q(Z^\dagger + 1),$$

where Q is some real constant; and

$$(18) \qquad \text{Case (ii):} \qquad Z^\dagger = 1,\ \Phi = 0, \text{ and } \Psi = 1 - |H|^2.$$

In case (i), with the definition,

$$E^\dagger = \frac{Z^\dagger - 1}{Z^\dagger + 1},$$ (19)

we find that $E^\dagger$ satisfies the equation,

$$(1 - 4Q^2 - |E|^2) \{[(1 - \eta^2)E,_\eta],_\eta - [(1 - \mu^2) E,_\mu],_\mu\}$$

$$= -2E^*[(1 - \eta^2) (E,_\eta)^2 - (1 - \mu^2) (E,_\mu)^2],$$ (20)

for *both* types of space-times we are presently considering. Moreover, it can be shown that if E_{vac} is a solution of the Ernst equation (9) for the vacuum, then

$$E_{\text{Ei,Ma}} = E_{\text{vac}} \sqrt{(1 - 4Q^2)}$$ (21)

is a solution of equation (20) appropriate for the Einstein-Maxwell equations. (It should be noted that in the stationary axisymmetric case, we should also consider the process of conjugation when the corresponding "tilded" variables will satisfy the same Ernst equation.)

In case (ii), we find that H satisfies the Ernst equation (9) for the vacuum so that we can write

$$H = E_{\text{vac}} \text{ and } \Psi = 1 - |E_{\text{vac}}|^2.$$ (22)

The completion of the solution for the various problems we shall consider, particularly in the theory of colliding waves, often requires fairly elaborate analysis. We shall not describe any of that analysis since it is not needed for exhibiting the structure and the coherence of the entire theory.

VIII

The origin of the structural similarity of the mathematical theory of black holes and colliding waves stems from the circumstance that in both cases the Einstein and the Einstein-Maxwell equations are reducible to the same Ernst equation; and indeed, as we shall see, even to the same solution. This identity is obtained only by the special choice of coordinates that assures the occurrence of an event horizon at a radial distance $\eta = 1$ for black holes and the development of a singularity at time $\eta = 1$ for colliding waves. The richness and the diversity of the physical situations that are described, in spite of this identity, results from the different combinations of the metric functions which can be associated with the same solution of the Ernst equation.

We shall consider first the solutions derived from the vacuum equations. The solution of the Ernst equation (9), from which the solutions describing the diverse physical situations follow, is the simplest one, namely,

$$(23) \qquad\qquad E = p\eta + iq\mu,$$

where p and q are two real constants restricted by the requirement,

$$(24) \qquad\qquad p^2 + q^2 = 1.$$

In the theory of black holes, the solution, $p\eta + iq\mu$, applies to $\tilde{E}^{\dagger}$, that is, to the Ernst equation for $\tilde{\Psi} + i\tilde{\Phi}$ belonging to the conjugate metric. The solution that follows is that of Kerr. It reduces to the Schwarzschild solution when $p = 1$ and $q = 0$. The resulting space-times of the Schwarzschild and the Kerr black-holes are adequately described in textbooks and are generally known. I shall mention only that these solutions belong to a special algebraic type, namely, type D in the Petrov classification. Solutions belonging to this type have many special properties. It is to these properties that we owe the separability of all the standard equations of mathematical physics in Kerr geometry.

Turning next to the theory of colliding waves, the fundamental solution is that of Khan and Penrose (1971) which describes the collision of two purely impulsive gravitational waves with parallel polarizations. It follows from the solution, $E = \eta$, of the Ernst equation for $\chi + iq_2$. The solution, $E = p\eta + iq\mu$, leads to the Nutku-Halil solution (1977) which describes the more general case when the colliding impulsive waves have nonparallel polarizations. Thus, the Khan-Penrose and the Nutku-Halil solutions play the same roles in the theory of colliding waves as the Schwarzschild and the Kerr solutions play in the theory of black holes.

The combination, $\Psi + i\Phi$, of the metric functions also leads to the same Ernst equation; and we are invited to consider the solution $p\eta + iq\mu$ for $E^{\dagger}$. The solution that follows has properties that were entirely unexpected: a horizon develops when $\eta = 1$, in place of a curvature singularity, violating a common belief that space-like curvature singularities are the rule when waves collide. In this instance, we must, therefore, extend the space-time beyond $\eta = 1$ and $|\mu| = 1$. When this extension is made, we find that the extended space-time includes a domain which is a mirror image of the one that was left behind and a further domain which includes hyperbolic arc-like singularities reminiscent of the ring singularity in the interior of the Kerr black-hole. It is remarkable that a space-time resulting from the collision of gravitational waves should bear such a close resemblance to Alice's anticipations with respect to the world *Through the Looking Glass:* "it [the passage in the Looking-Glass House] is very like our passage as far as you can see, only it may be quite different on beyond."

The foregoing remarks, concerning the solution derived from $E^\dagger = p\eta + iq\mu$, apply only when $q \neq 0$. When $q = 0$ and $p = 1$, a space-like curvature singularity develops at $\eta = 1$; and the space-time cannot be extended into the future.

Finally, it should be noted that the solution derived from $E^\dagger = p\eta + iq\mu$ is of type D and shares all the mathematical features of space-times belonging to this type.

Turning next to the Einstein-Maxwell equations, we are led to the solutions appropriate to charged black-holes when we consider the solution $E = p\eta + iq\mu$ $(p^2 + q^2 = 1 - 4Q^2)$ for the Ernst equation (20) for $\tilde{E}^\dagger$, in accordance with equation (21). We obtain the Reissner-Nordstrom solution when $q = 0$, and the Kerr-Newman solution when $q \neq 0$.

There were conceptual difficulties in obtaining the corresponding "elementary" solutions of the Einstein-Maxwell equations for colliding waves. Penrose had raised the question: would an impulsive gravitational wave with its associated δ-function singularity in the Weyl tensor imply a similar δ-function singularity in the Maxwell tensor? If that should happen, then the expression for the electromagnetic field-variables would involve the square root of the δ-function; and "one would be at a loss to know how to interpret such a function." Besides, there was the formidable problem of satisfying the many boundary conditions at the various null boundaries. On these accounts, all efforts to obtain solutions compatible with carefully formulated initial conditions failed. However, when it was realized that the Khan-Penrose and the Nutku-Halil solutions followed from the simplest solution of the Ernst equation for $\chi + iq_2$, it was natural to seek a solution of the Einstein-Maxwell equations which will reduce to the Nutku-Halil solution when the Maxwell field is switched off. The problem is not a straightforward one: since, in the framework of the Einstein-Maxwell equations, we do not have an Ernst equation at the level of the metric functions χ and q_2: we have one only for $E^\dagger$ derived for $\Psi + i\Phi + |H|^2$. The technical problems that are presented can be successfully overcome and a solution can be obtained which satisfies all the necessary boundary conditions and physical requirements. That we can obtain a physically consistent solution by this "inverted procedure" is a manifestation of the firm aesthetic base of the general theory of relativity.

Since we do have an Ernst equation for $\Psi + i\Phi + |H|^2$, we can consider the solution $E = p\eta + iq\mu$ $(p^2 + q^2 = 1 - 4Q^2)$, for the Ernst equation (20) for $E^\dagger$. When $Q = 0$, this solution will reduce to the solution for the vacuum we have described earlier; and we find that, like the vacuum solution, it develops a horizon and, subsequently, time-like singularities.

In our consideration of the Einstein-Maxwell equations in § VII, we have distinguished two cases: case (i) and case (ii). They differ in essential ways: when the electromagnetic field is switched off, the space-time, in case (i), reduces to a nontrivial solution of the Einstein vacuum-equations, while in case (ii), it becomes flat. The solutions we have considered hitherto belong to case (i). As we have seen, in case (ii) the complex electromagnetic potential, H, satisfies the Ernst equation (9) for the vacuum. We naturally ask the nature of the space-time that will follow from the simplest solution, $p\eta + iq\mu$, of the Ernst equation. The solution one then obtains (discovered by Bell and Szekeres by different methods) is a very remarkable one: gravitation, as manifested by a nonvanishing Weyl scalar, is confined exclusively to the δ-function profile describing the impulsive gravitational waves. In other words, except for the presence of the impulsive waves, the space-time is conformally flat. Thus, as an exact solution of the Einstein-Maxwell equations, we have a conformally flat space-time in which plane-fronted electromagnetic shock-waves, accompanying impulsive gravitational waves, collide and develop a horizon. A further feature of the Bell-Szekeres solution (1974) is that the solution for $q = 0$ is entirely equivalent to the solution for $q \neq 0$. Therefore, to obtain a solution in this framework which will describe a more general physical situation than the Bell-Szekeres solution, we must go outside the range of the simplest solution of the Ernst equation. For this purpose, we take advantage of a transformation due to Ehlers which enables us to obtain a one-parameter family of solutions from any given solution of the Ernst equation. We therefore consider the Ehlers transform of the solution, $E = p\eta + iq\mu$. We find that the resulting solutions are of type D and have all the features of the solution for the vacuum derived from the solution $E^\dagger = p\eta + iq\mu$. It is remarkable that we should obtain a one-parameter family of space-times with this abundant structure by applying the Ehlers transformation to the Bell-Szekeres solution.

In table 1 we describe more fully the various solutions that have been derived for black holes and for colliding waves. The pictorial pattern of this table is a visible manifestation of the structural unity of the subject.

The inner relationships between the theory of black holes and the theory of colliding waves is equally visible (see table 2) in the simpler context when $\omega = 0$ and $q_2 = 0$. In this case, the basic equation on which the solutions for both theories depend is

$$[(1 - \eta^2)\,(\lg\Psi),_\eta],_\eta - [(1 - \mu^2)\,(\lg\Psi),_\mu],_\mu = 0. \qquad (25)$$

This equation can be solved exactly, and the solutions that are relevant in the two theories are listed in table 2.

As the foregoing discussion demonstrates, the Einstein-Maxwell equations share many of the distinctive features of the Einstein vacuum-equations. The only source, other than a Maxwell field, which when coupled with gravitation leads to equations which retain at least some of the distinctive features of the vacuum equations, is a perfect fluid with the equation of state, energy-density (ϵ) = pressure (p). For such a fluid, the Ricci tensor, in accordance with Einstein's equations, is given by

$$R^{ij} = -4\epsilon\, u^i u^j, \qquad (26)$$

where u^i denotes the four-velocity of the fluid.

On the assumption that in the region of the interaction of the colliding waves, *after* the instant of collision, we have as source a perfect fluid with $\epsilon = p$, we find that, *prior* to the instant of collision, the impulsive gravitational waves *must* have been accompanied by null dust with an energy-momentum tensor of the form,

$$T^{ij} = Ek^i k^j = -\tfrac{1}{2}R^{ij}, \qquad (27)$$

where E is some positive scalar function and k^i denotes a null vector. In other words, under the circumstances envisaged, a transformation of null dust (i.e., massless particles describing null trajectories) into a perfect fluid (whose stream lines follow time-like trajectories) occurs at the instant of collision. That such a transformation is required is, in the first instance, surprising. But as Roger Penrose and Lee Lindblom have pointed out, the transformation in question can take place, equally, in the framework of special relativity though this fact does not seem to have been noticed before.

In developing the theory of colliding waves in parallel with the theory of black holes, we have, in effect, examined systematically the consequences of adopting for the Ernst equation, in its various contexts, its simplest solution (or, in one case, its Ehlers transform). While this approach may appear as an exceedingly formal one, it has nevertheless disclosed possibilities that one could not have in any way foreseen, as for example, the development of horizons and subsequent time-like singularities or the transformation of null dust into a perfect fluid. In this instance, then, exploring general relativity, sensitive to its aesthetic base, has led to a deepening of our understanding of the *physical* content of the theory.

Table 1

Killing Vectors	Field Equations	Solution for Ernst Equation for		
		E	$E^\dagger$	$\tilde{E}^\dagger$
$\partial_t, \partial_\phi$	Einstein-vacuum	does not exist		η
$\partial_t, \partial_\phi$	Einstein-vacuum	does not exist		$p\eta + iq\mu; p^2 + q^2 =$
$\partial_t, \partial_\phi$	Einstein-Maxwell	does not exist		$\eta\sqrt{(1-4Q^2)}$
$\partial_t, \partial_\phi$	Einstein-Maxwell	does not exist		$p\eta + iq\mu;$ $p^2 + q^2 = 1-4Q$
$\partial_{x^1}, \partial_{x^2}$	Einstein-vacuum	η		interchanges x^1 and x^2
$\partial_{x^1}, \partial_{x^2}$	Einstein-vacuum	$p\eta + iq\mu;$ $p^2 + q^2 = 1$		interchanges x^1 and x^2
$\partial_{x^1}, \partial_{x^2}$	Einstein-Maxwell	does not exist	$E^\dagger (E_{vac} = p\eta + iq\mu)$ $\times \sqrt{(1-4Q^2)})$	interchanges x^1 and x^2
$\partial_{x^1}, \partial_{x^2}$	Einstein-vacuum		η	interchanges x^1 and x^2
$\partial_{x^1}, \partial_{x^2}$	Einstein-vacuum		$p\eta + iq\mu; p^2 + q^2 = 1$	interchanges x^1 and x^2
$\partial_{x^1}, \partial_{x^2}$	Einstein-Maxwell	does not exist	$\eta\sqrt{(1-4Q^2)}$	interchanges x^1 and x^2

Solution	Description
Schwarzschild	Black hole; static; spherically symmetric event horizon space-like singularity at center type D; parameter: mass
Kerr	Black hole; stationary, axisymmetric event & Cauchy horizons; ergosphere time-like ring-singularity in equatorial plane type D; parameters: mass and angular momentum
Reissner-Nordström	Charged black-hole; static; spherically symmetric event and Cauchy horizons time-like singularity at center type D; parameters: mass and charge
Kerr-Newman	Charged black-hole; stationary, axisymmetric event & Cauchy horizons: ergosphere time-like ring-singularity in equatorial plane type D; parameters: mass, charge, and angular momentum
Khan-Penrose	Collision of impulsive gravitational waves parallel polarizations develops space-like curvature singularity
Nutku-Halil	Collision of impulsive gravitational waves nonparallel polarizations develops space-like curvature singularity (weaker than Khan-Penrose)
Chandrasekhar and Xanthopoulos	Collision of impulsive gravitational waves and accompanying gravitational and electromagnetic shock-waves nonparallel polarizations develops space-like curvature singularity
Chandrasekhar and Xanthopoulos	Collision of impulsive gravitational waves and accompanying gravitational shock-waves parallel polarizations develops very strong space-like curvature singularity type D
Chandrasekhar and Xanthopoulos	Collision of impulsive gravitational waves and accompanying gravitational shock-waves nonparallel polarizations develops a horizon and subsequent time-like arc-singularities type D
Chandrasekhar and Xanthopoulos	Collision of impulsive gravitational waves and accompanying gravitational and electromagnetic shock-waves parallel polarizations develops a horizon and subsequent three-dimensional time-like arc-singularities type D

TABLE 1 *continued*

Killing Vectors	Field Equations	Solution for Ernst Equation for		
		E	$E^\dagger$	$\bar{E}^\dagger$
$\partial_{x^1}, \partial_{x^2}$	Einstein-Maxwell	does not exist	$p\eta + iq\mu$; $p^2 + q^2 = 1 - 4Q^2$	interchanges x^1 and x^2
$\partial_{x^1}, \partial_{x^2}$	Einstein-Maxwell $(H = E_{\text{vac}})$	does not exist	η	interchanges x^1 and x^2
$\partial_{x^1}, \partial_{x^2}$	Einstein-Maxwell $(H = E_{\text{vac}})$	does not exist	$p\eta + iq\mu$; $p^2 + q^2 = 1$	interchanges x^1 and x^2
$\partial_{x^1}, \partial_{x^2}$	Einstein-Maxwell $(H = E_{\text{vac}})$	does not exist	Ehlers transform of $p\eta + iq\mu$	interchanges x^1 and x^2
$\partial_{x^1}, \partial_{x^2}$	Einstein-hydrodynamics $(\epsilon = p)$	$p\eta + iq\mu$		interchanges x^1 and x^2

In his first announcement of his field equations in November 1915, Einstein concluded with the statement:

Anyone who fully comprehends this theory cannot escape its magic.

At least to one practitioner, the magic of the theory is in the harmonious coherence of its mathematical structure.

APPENDIX

On 29 June 1916, Einstein gave a brief memorial address on Karl Schwarzschild at a meeting of the Berliner Akademie. It presents a proper measure of Schwarzschild, and I have thought it worthwhile to append the following translation of Einstein's address.

On May 11 of this year [1916], Karl Schwarzschild, 42 years old, was by death, snatched away. This early demise of so gifted and many-sided a scientist is a grievous loss not only to this body, but also to all his astronomer and physicist friends.

What is specially astonishing about Schwarzschild's theoretical work is his easy command of mathematical methods and the almost casual way in which

Solution	Description
Chandrasekhar and Xanthopoulos	Collision of impulsive gravitational waves and accompanying gravitational and electromagnetic shock-waves nonparallel polarizations develops a horizon and subsequent time-like arc-singularities type D
Bell-Szekeres	Collision of impulsive gravitational waves and accompanying electromagnetic shock-waves parallel polarizations space-time conformally flat develops a horizon; permits extension with no subsequent singularities
Bell-Szekeres	Same as above
Chandrasekhar and Xanthopoulos	Collision of impulsive gravitational waves and accompanying gravitational and electromagnetic shock-waves develops a horizon and subsequent time-like arc-singularities type D
Chandrasekhar and Xanthopoulos	Collision of impulsive gravitational and accompanying gravitational shock-waves and null dust $(R_{ij} = Ck_ik_j)$ nonparallel polarizations develops weakened space-like singularity transforms null dust into a perfect fluid with $\epsilon = p$

he could penetrate to the essence of astronomical or physical questions. Rarely has so much mathematical erudition been adapted to reasoning about physical reality. And so it was, that he grappled with many problems from which others shrank away on account of mathematical difficulties. The mainsprings of Schwarzschild's motivations in his restless theoretical quests seem less from a curiosity to learn the deeper inner relationships among the different aspects of Nature than from an artist's delight in discerning delicate mathematical patterns. It is therefore understandable that Schwarzschild's earliest contributions were in celestial mechanics, a branch of science whose foundations are more firmly established than any other. In this area, I may recall his investigations on the periodic solutions of the three-body problem and Poincaré's theory of the equilibrium of rotating fluid masses.

Among the most important of Schwarzschild's astronomical contributions are his investigations on stellar statistics, i.e., a part of science which seeks by statistical methods to relate the observations on the luminosity, the velocity, and the spectral type of stars to the structure of a large system of many objects to which the sun belongs. In this area, astronomers are indebted to him for deepening and widening their understanding of Kapteyn's discovery.

Schwarzschild directed his deep knowledge of theoretical physics to the theory of the sun. Here, one is grateful for his investigations on the equilib-

TABLE 2

Killing Vectors	Field Equations	Solution	Remarks
$\partial_t, \partial_\phi$	Einstein vacuum	$\ln \tilde{\Psi} = \ln \dfrac{\eta-1}{\eta+1}$	Schwarschild solution: spherically symmetric static black-hole
$\partial_t, \partial_\phi$	Einstein vacuum	$\ln \tilde{\Psi} = \ln \dfrac{\eta-1}{\eta+1} + \sum_n A_n P_n(\mu) P_n(\eta)$	*Distorted black-holes (when* $\sum A_{2n+1} P_{2n+1}$ (1) $= 0$); Weyl's solutions
$\partial_{x^1}, \partial_{x^2}$	Einstein vacuum	$\ln \chi = \ln \dfrac{1+\eta}{1-\eta}$	Khan-Penrose solution for colliding impulsive waves with parallel polarizations
$\partial_{x^1}, \partial_{x^2}$	Einstein vacuum	$\ln \chi = \ln \dfrac{1+\eta}{1-\eta} + \sum_n A_n P_n(\mu) P_n(\eta)$	Collision of impulsive gravitational waves with accompanying gravitational shock-waves; parallel polarizations
$\partial_{x^1}, \partial_{x^2}$	Einstein-Maxwell ($H = E_{\text{vac}}$)	$\dfrac{1}{2} \ln \dfrac{1+H}{1-H} = \dfrac{1}{2} \ln \dfrac{1+\eta}{1-\eta}$	Collision of impulsive gravitational waves with accompanying electromagnetic shock-waves in conformally flat space-time; parallel polarizations; Bell-Szekeres solution
$\partial_{x^1}, \partial_{x^2}$	Einstein-Maxwell ($H = E_{\text{vac}}$)	$\dfrac{1}{2} \ln \dfrac{1+H}{1-H} = \dfrac{1}{2} \ln \dfrac{1+\eta}{1-\eta} + \sum_n A_n P_n(\mu) P_n(\eta)$	Collision of impulsive gravitational waves with accompanying gravitational and electromagnetic shock-waves; parallel polarizations

NOTE: Basic equation, $[(1-\eta^2) \, (\ln\psi)_{,\eta}]_{,\eta} - [(1-\mu^2) \, (\ln\psi)_{,\mu}]_{,\mu} = 0$

rium of the solar atmosphere and for considerations relating to radiative transfer. To this area also belong his beautiful investigations on the pressure of light on small spherical particles which provided an exact basis for Arrhenius's theory of comet tails. These investigations in theoretical physics, while they were motivated by astronomical questions, seem to have led Schwarzschild to be interested in questions purely in physics. We are indebted to him for his interesting contributions to the foundations of electrodynamics. Besides, in his last year he became interested in the new theory of gravitation: he succeeded in obtaining, for the first time, an exact calculation in the new theory of gravitation. And in the very last months of his life, much weakened by a fell disease, he yet succeeded in making some profound contributions to quantum theory.

To Schwarzschild's great theoretical contributions also belong his investigations on geometrical optics in which he refined the theory of aberrations of optical instruments of astronomical importance. These studies will remain an enduring edifice for the perfection of the tools of astronomy.

Schwarzschild's theoretical investigations were carried out simultaneously with his efforts as a practical astronomer. From age 24, he worked at observatories without interruption: 1896–99 as an assistant in Wien; 1901–9 as Director of the Göttingen Observatory; and after 1909 as Director of the Astrophysical Institute at Potsdam. A long series of investigations testify to his efforts as an observer and as a leader of astronomical observations. Moreover, his lively spirit led him to advance his scientific field by charting new methods of observation. He discovered, in experimental physics, what has been named after him, how the blackening of a photographic plate can be used for the purposes of photometry by photographic methods. He also had the brilliant idea of using extra-focal images of stars for measuring their brightness: only through this idea did photographic photometry, besides visual methods, become feasible.

Since 1912, this modest man has been a member of this Akademie to whose *Sitzungsberichte* he has, in this short time, communicated many important contributions. Now bitter circumstances have taken him away: but his work will bear fruits and have an enduring influence on Science for which he devoted all his strength.

REFERENCES

The nature of this lecture precludes giving a list of references in conventional style. However, the particular papers of Karl Schwarzschild quoted explicitly in the text are:

"Bemerkung zür Elektrodynamik," *Phys. Zeits.* **4** (1903): 431.
"Ueber die Eigenbewegungen der Fixterne," *Göttinger Nachrichten,* 1907, p. 614.
"Ueber das zulässige Krümmungsmass des Raumes," *Vierteljahrsschrift der Astronomischen Gesellschaft* **35** (1900): 337.

"Über das Gravitationsfeld eines Massenpunktes nach der Einsteinschen Theorie," *Sitzungsberichte* (Berliner Akademie), 3 February 1916, p. 189.

"Über das Gravitationsfeld einer Kugel aus inkompressibler Flüssigkeit nach der Einsteinschen Theorie," *Sitzungsberichte* (Berliner Akademie), 23 March 1916, p. 424.

"Zür Quantenhypothese," *Sitzungsberichte* (Berliner Akademie), 4 May 1916, p. 548.

Referring to Schwarzschild's paper "Bemerkung zür Elektrodynamik," C. Lanczos (in *The Einstein Decade* [New York and London: Academic Press, 1974], p. 152) comments, "Schwarzschild's remarkable anticipation of the relativistically invariant proper formulation of the principle of least action is not recorded in any history of physics."

For an account of Schwarzschild's contributions to the notions of action and angle variables, see:

Sommerfeld, A., *Atombau und Spektrallinien,* vol. 1, 5th ed. (Braunschweig: Vieweg & Sohn, 1931), pp. 659–63.

The discussion of the theory of black holes and of colliding waves in §§ VI–VIII is based on:

Chandrasekhar, S., *The Mathematical Theory of Black Holes* (Oxford: Clarendon Press, 1983).

Khan, K., and Penrose, R., *Nature, Lond.* **229**, 185 (1971).

Nutku, Y., and Halil, M., *Phys. Rev. Lett.* **39**, 1379 (1977).

Bell, P., and Szekeres, P., *Gen. Rel. Grav.* **5**, 275 (1974).

Chandrasekhar, S., and Ferrari, V., *Proc. Roy. Soc. Lond.* **A396**, 55 (1984).

Chandrasekhar, S., and Xanthopoulos, X., *Proc. Roy. Soc. Lond.* **A398**, 223 (1985); **A402**, 37 (1985); **A403**, 189 (1985); **A408**, 175 (1986); and **A410** 311 (1987).